Putting the Cart Before the Dog?

BILL MOORE

Copyright © 2017 Bill Moore

All rights reserved.

ISBN:1548003999
ISBN-13:978-1548003999

The information contained within this book is strictly for educational purposes. If you wish to apply ideas contained in this book, you are taking full responsibility for your actions.

DEDICATION

For my beautiful wife

Acknowledgements

Thank you, Melisa, for the encouragement, inspiration and editing. You made this all possible.

Thank you to:

Ed Ourant, the man who gave me a chance by changing corporate policy.

Mark Caserta, my friend whose leadership style I still teach thirty-something years later.

Dave Thomas, who taught me to stand up for what I believed and fight for making operations better.

Mark Ordway, the most principled operator I've ever met. If he said it, it happened, and it was right.

Preface

    Another book about starting a hot dog business? There are already a few dozen that cover the subject with varying degrees of useful information. Some are written by professional writers giving basic information from internet research that a high school student would perform for a term paper. A couple are written by CPAs and CISAs steeped in theory and over-complicated mathematics. Others are written by ex-vendors that have moved on to other hot dog cart related endeavors using the book platform as a marketing device to sell whatever else they are hawking. Still others are written from limited experience as a vendor (a year or two) giving an unrealistic view of the food industry as being easy and implying exaggerated potential income for those that just "give it a try." These writers often offer free email and video "training" hoping to hook you into buying something else from them such as a cart, DIY plans, a website or a private group with "secrets" to share.

    I write from decades of experience in the food industry as well as street vending. I want to provide a realistic overview of vending without all the rah-rah of a person with something to sell beyond this book. My approach is real world with numbers based on my experience, not theory or research. I will call out incorrect and misleading information as I find it, not to glorify my experience but to encourage revision and accuracy. The food industry has been my entire adult life. I respect it and want to train others to be successful in this challenging, yet rewarding industry.

The title "Putting the Cart Before the Dog?" is an observation of how most folks dive into food vending and subsequently fail. Focusing on purchasing a piece of equipment first instead of researching and developing a sound business plan featuring a delicious product delivered in an efficient, guest-centric method. Imagine Dave Thomas buying land, building a beautiful building full of amazing equipment and then saying, "Ok boys, now what do we sell?"

If you have a positive attitude and constantly strive to give your best effort, eventually you will overcome your immediate problems and find you are ready for greater challenges. **Pat Riley**

Table of Contents

Acknowledgements **v**

Preface **vi**

Who Is This Guy??! - **1** -

Sales Pitches Vs Truth - **6** -

TO DO Lists - **13** -

RESEARCH - **18** -

MENU - **27** -

SUPPLIERS - **57** -

LOCATION - **72** -

EQUIPMENT - **86** -

LICENSES - **99** -

MENTOR - **109** -

Operations - **112** -

Marketing - **135** -

All About You - **144** -

Starting with Nothing - **151** -

Expansion Time! - **158** -

Glossary - **166** -

Excuses, excuses - **171** -

Links - **178** -

Who Is This Guy??!

The day you find out who you are is when you look back and realize that it was never the words, rather your actions that defined you. **Shannon L. Alder**

> **Warning: Mandatory Rags to Riches Tale**
>
> "I lost my job at *(fill in the blank industry that has nothing to do with food service)* and I had no savings and was on food stamps about to lose my house when I scraped, begged and borrowed my way to a cart and started selling hot dogs on a snowy mountain that I had to push the cart uphill 5 miles to each day as dumb as a rock, basically lazy and made every mistake possible, but now I am financially set and now I want to share my mistakes so you don't suffer like I did. I will a) teach {read 'sell'} you a course how to do the same thing just join my "pro" fellowship for only $$$, b) sell you plans to build your own cart based on 1926 patent designs, c) sell you one of my best in the industry, work flow inefficient, massively overpriced carts."

Who Is This Guy?

How often do you go internet surfing and an ad catches your eye? You click on it and discover an inspiring story complete with a hard luck tales written by the comeback kid himself. Rising like a phoenix from the ashes of a failed business, lost job or corporate "downsizing" this self-made protagonist of the ad is ready to share (meaning SELL) his story, his easy to follow plans or offer his expertise to you for a pittance. After reading about a million words of self-denigration followed closely by the phoenix story and "unsolicited" testimonials you get to the crux of the ad, the price. Depending on how emotionally invested you are in the story you may find yourself impulse buying the plans, membership or merchandise being offered.

Rags to Riches stories are so inspiring but often more on the "fisherman's tale" side of reality. We, as emotional beings, remember ads that touch us in some manner and then connect that warm, fuzzy feeling to the product. We have made an emotional decision rather than a logical one. Ads that make an emotional connection to the viewer result in higher, more frequent sales. Ad copywriters are fantastic at doing that by using extremely descriptive words and images to make emotional connection. There is a direct correlation to ad wordiness and product usefulness or value. The longer the ad the more expensive the product. Remember expensive does not equal value or quality.

My tale is simple, I have decades of experience with the restaurant industry big boys. I owned hot dog concession stands that average $425.00 in profit a day as well as operated restaurants ranging in sales from $300,000 to $5 million in sales a year. (In case you are wondering it was the Wendy's in St Thomas US Virgin Islands. Yes, the one at the end of the cruise ship dock in Havensight). I have, in person, dealt with dozens of health inspectors in 7 different states and the USVI. I have worked in nearly 60 different locations and have restaurant headhunters and previous employers chasing me (in a good way). I have been on the front line dealing with employees, guests, food costs and profits for Rax Restaurants, Wendy's, Shoney's, Hardees, Burger King, Whataburger, McDonalds, Quiznos and Schlotzsky's and still found time to operate my hot dog carts. I know a thing or two because I've lived it for 40 years!

My parents and grandparents all worked and worked hard. No complaints. My grandfather was always teaching us whether we realized it or not. Every Sunday he would go to the church in the early morning to light the coal stove so by service time the room was nice and toasty. He was always working at something be it the garden (growing enough food to eat as well as store for the winter), with neighbors or at the hardware store. Grandpa often volunteered when people need help such as major flooding in areas like Pikeville or across the state line in Virginia. I once asked why he helped people he often didn't even know, and he replied, "The Bible says, **'Do not forget to do good and to help one another, because these are the sacrifices that please God.'** _They need help, so I do what needs to be done._" Some 46 years later I still try to follow his example. I want to help you achieve your dream of business ownership, no strings attached. You have been taught nothing in life is free. Well, this is! Outside of the pittance you paid for this book I won't ask for any more money. I will link YouTube videos, checklists and spreadsheets that you can view and download for free. I won't spend 2500 words getting you hooked into this business and then pull the rug out from under you by telling you the real secrets or insider information is behind a pay wall of $$$$$.

By the end of reading this book and following the action steps, you will know how to own and operate a profitable hot dog vending business. I am going to give you actionable information that will get you started in the food industry as a hot dog vendor. I am going to give you the full enchilada, as it were, of information, help, tips and warnings. By the time you are finished doing your part of the work you will know what your state requires, how to set up a

Who Is This Guy?

profitable menu, how to buy a used cart and how to market your business. I will even throw in a *legal plan* for starting with less than $50 and growing it until you can afford a cart and expand your business.

Ready to learn? This business does require research on your part. No one, and I mean no one, is an expert on all 50 states' heath department requirements. State laws are in constant flux. Interpretations of rules, changes in food categories and county enforcement all change and change often. In many cases, local officials can't even agree on inspections and how to score them. All too often one inspector says one thing and another inspector 6 months later says the opposite. Some cart sellers that brag about having all 50 states codes, I say "good for you, buddy". Now ask them if they are on the mailing list for state code updates and interpretation memos. Or mailing lists for all 3,144 county health departments in the US. Or talked, in person, with an inspector about changes coming to inspections 6 months down the road. Or receive the daily recall memos from USDA. Guess what, codes are online, technically we **all** have them! This link has them all listed so now you can brag about "having all 50 state codes", too! https://www.fda.gov/Food/GuidanceRegulation/RetailFoodProtection/FoodCode/ucm122814.htm

One would think a cart selling training "pro" would know there are actually 66 state level agencies that regulate restaurants or retail food stores. All but 2 have adopted the FDA Food Code, only varying which year they have adopted. Once you have read the 1995 version and all the change memos from 1997, 1999, 2001, 2005, 2009, 2013 and the upcoming one in 2017, you will have ALMOST all of the state codes. You will have to go to New York and Vermont to finish your study of state codes. Now while each state has adopted the FDA code from different years as a basis for their own codes each state will then change, tweak, delete or add to the code making it fit in with their own existing laws. Then the county steps in and

does more modifications in several states. Guess what, some cities even add more regulations! The braggart "pro" claiming knowledge of all 50 state codes is way short of being able to brag. Here is the breakdown of codes per state agency:
https://www.fda.gov/downloads/Food/GuidanceRegulation/RetailFoodProtection/FoodCode/UCM577858.pdf

  Luckily, you only need to be an expert in your **location and state**. I won't link state web pages as they change often. Just look at some of the cart manufacturer sites, check the links and you will find several broken ones. It is just easier to give search terms and hit enter on your search engine. If you are having trouble finding the correct information or understanding the regulations just email or call me and we can search together.

Sales Pitches Vs Truth

You were born to win, but to be a winner, you must plan to win, you must prepare to win, and then and only then can you expect to win.
Zig Ziglar

Your jaw will drop when you see how easy it is to make money!

Industry giants shocked when man reveals insider secrets!

Learn the secrets THEY don't want you to know!

Did I cover all the click bait nonsense? The headlines designed to draw you in and hook you into spending money that perhaps you don't have. The articles that reveal absolutely nothing, your jaw remains closed, you didn't even feel a tingle of a shock and the secrets aren't even secret. I see these every day and so do you. I avoid every article that has these types of headlines. It indicates there is no substance to what they are writing and often no expertise behind the words. But, what has made me angry is these charlatans have invaded my industry. My blood boils when I see information that is vague, incorrect or misleading all in the name of selling you a cart, DIY build a cart plan or selling membership in some nonsense "pro" group.

Putting the Cart Before the Dog

When you search "hot dog cart business" on the internet you will no doubt run across manufacturers sites but also several distinct "personalities" that have various wares to sell connected with hot dog selling. Unless you are very familiar with running a restaurant, it is very scary thinking about starting a food cart or truck. Armed with this knowledge, these aforementioned charlatans prey on would be entrepreneurs with "free" training that is nothing more than generalized hype understating real world difficulties or just flat out WRONG. The training and websites pummel you with repetitive ads on every page, email gathering tricks and other browser high jacking marketing tricks left over from the 1990's and AOL. One dude claims to be the "Hot Dog" King, wears a crown and acts like a used cars salesman from 1970. Yet another guy hypes everything hot dog while attempting to sell you membership to his vendor only group under the guise of "free training" and provides live Facebook "updates" that often contain incorrect food service information. When challenged to correct wrong information, either deletes the challenge comment or the complete video then reposts the same video with sanitized comments but leaving the incorrect information intact. Another uses near daily contact via email. His trick Du jour is pretending to answer a question from one of his followers, of course the answer can only be seen on his website rather than in the email with the supposed question. This, in and of itself, demonstrates gross inefficiency no real business person would exercise. BUT a **salesman** on the other hand, would. The answers are vague, generalities offering no real assistance but to an outsider to the food industry the answer could seem substantive.

Each of these guys have a common hard luck story, followed by a vending saved me from ruin story. Amazingly each one stopped vending fairly soon (a year or two) after starting their carts and began either selling carts or selling plans to build carts at home or selling both. Saying I am a little disturbed by these carpetbagging food "pro" wannabes would be an understatement. Enough about them. Enough about me. Time to focus on YOU!

Let me tell you, right now, the real restaurant business well-kept secret and I'll tell you for **free!**

(TRAINING x PRACTICE) + (LOCATION x HARD WORK) = SUCCESS.

There you go. That is, it. If there were "secrets" wouldn't the big guys like McDonalds or Wendy's have a team of lawyers preventing those secrets from leaking out to the masses? Look at how Prince protected his music during his lifetime from being posted on streaming sites and YouTube. Don't think for one second the same wouldn't happen if real "secrets" existed and were then being revealed.

These "hot dog slinging pros" training may have some value but will be far from earth shattering "secrets". Anyone that has worked in a time conscious environment (like, ummm, I don't know ... FAST FOOD) has no patience for rambling, wordy ads or videos. Give me the facts without the fluff and I can make a good decision, no persuasion tricks needed.

The message of the sales pitch is designed to get you excited. They tell stories of the $100,000 a year income working only three hours a day. My calculator says $100,000 divided by 52 weeks is $1923.08. Working only Friday, Saturday and Sunday that is 9 hours at $213.68 an hour, right? Well, no its not. Any restaurant operation (that is really what a hot dog cart is) has prep and clean up time. So, either the 3 hours is only service time, meaning your day is more likely 4 to 6 hours or you are selling food only 1 or 2 hours. You also must source and purchase your supplies which also adds time to your routine. They, also, FAIL to mention the $100,000 is gross sales not bottom line after taxes profit.

Profit and Loss Statement

Income

Gross Sales	$	100,000.00
Sales Tax	$	5,660.38
Net sales	$	94,339.62
Credit Card Sales	$	11,670.00

Variable Costs

Food and Paper

Open Inv	$	450.50	
Purchases	$	27,607.72	
Ending Inv	$	58.22	
Subtotal Food & Paper	$	28,000.00	29.68%

Operational

Gasoline	$	615.00	0.65%
Propane	$	1,205.50	1.28%
Cleaning	$	247.32	0.26%
CC Processing fees	$	320.93	0.34%
Marketing	$	205.10	0.22%
Ice	$	425.00	0.45%
			0.00%
			0.00%
			0.00%
			0.00%
Total Variable Costs	$	31,018.85	32.88%

Fixed Costs

Commissary Fee	$	3,000.00	3.18%
Telephone	$	540.00	0.57%
Rent	$	3,000.00	3.18%
Insurance General	$	400.00	0.42%
Licenses/Inspection fees	$	597.00	0.63%
Bank Charges	$	120.00	0.13%
			0.00%
			0.00%
			0.00%
			0.00%
Total Fixed Costs	$	7,657.00	8.12%
Profit/Loss	$	55,663.77	59.00%

Breakeven	$	11,407.92

Sales Pitches Vs Truth

Every business has a "breakeven" point. That is the point where all the fixed costs are covered and the variable costs to achieve that exact level of sales is also covered. In the example P&L on the next page, you can see the fixed and variable costs of a hot dog cart. You will also see the breakeven point. On the road to $100,000 in sales the first $11,407.92 in sales is just to breakeven for the year. That means zero profit. BUT on the remainder of the sales you are only having to pay for materials that directly or indirectly go in the finished product for your guests. All your profit is here! $55,663.78 or 59%, amazing numbers BUT still not all yours. You have taxes to pay. Self-employment, income, FICA and business taxes all come out of this figure. Don't worry you will still have a good income for the days worked. It is just nowhere near that $100,000 point the "pro" cart selling pretend trainers brag about. The P&L on page 9 is set up using a more realistic working days total of 141 a year. You could work more, and weather could force you to work less.

Using the same cost percentages and work days to clear $100,000 a year in profit would require net sales (gross less sales taxes) of $169,731.17 or $1203.77 a day. A consistent $1200 day is possible with the right location and work ethic, but sadly these are the exceptions not the rule. As you can see, emotional stories and hype often create an impulse purchase of courses, clubs, and carts.

If you have never seen a restaurant P&L before generally there are a lot more lines and a lot more categories. Most of today's restaurant managers have no idea how to figure costs. A computer or in many cases the cash register tells a manager food, supply and labor costs. Today's fast food managers are highly paid food service workers with no clue how much money the company makes or loses. If you are a fast food manager today, please don't be offended, it is not your fault. Franchise owners mask the P&L as much as possible to hide personal income. If you work for the franchisor they make more money off real estate, license fees, royalties and marketing fees than the stores they operate. Both franchisee and franchisor will teach food, paper, supplies and labor controls. Most managers are generally measured and then bonused on these areas, so that is all they worry about.

If you can answer these questions and you actively work to improve these areas in your restaurant, then consider yourself an expert! If you want a detailed explanation email me and I will explain!

- ➢ How does the demand meter impact your P&L?
- ➢ How much is your workman's comp premium and how do you impact it?
- ➢ Name any equipment that is water cooled and how does that impact your water bill?
- ➢ What supplier/manufacturer rebates does your restaurant receive and where is it credited on your P&L?
- ➢ How much is your unemployment tax and is it controllable at the store level?
- ➢ How are workman's comp premiums effected by accidents?
- ➢ What is the difference in a fixed cost and a variable cost?
- ➢ What is direct and indirect labor?
- ➢ What part of a freezer/cooler is actually heated?
- ➢ When were the O-rings were replaced on your shake or ice cream machine?
- ➢ Why does the ice machine drain line clog and how to prevent clogging?
- ➢ Where is the cooking oil recovery rebate credited on your P&L?

Sales Pitches Vs Truth

- How many cubic yards does your dumpster hold and is it nearly full when picked up <u>every time</u>?
- Is it more cost effective to have a larger dumpster picked up less times, or a small dumpster picked up more often?
- Could you manually figure food cost without aid of a computer?

You get the point. Few mangers will know all the answers but a so-called "good" manager will know last week's food and labor costs as well as today's lunch SOS (speed of service). You **can** still go bankrupt controlling only those numbers.

Bottom line - running a hot dog cart is work and often hard, hot, very physically tiring work. Can you succeed? Absolutely! All you must do is set yourself up for success. Starting your business is simply a series of questions requiring answers. The better the answers, the stronger the business and the greater likelihood of success. The starting point is following the TO DO lists in the next chapter. Everything in this book is geared toward the necessary research to write your business plan. I even have an example business plan for a cart you can download at https://moorebetterperformance.weebly.com/downloads.html That is what this book, all my videos and documents are trying to do, help you develop a written plan for success. Best of all I will help you with anything you don't understand!

TO DO Lists

Lists are how I parse and manage the world. **Adam Savage**

According to the Small Business Administration there are 10 steps to opening a successful business. We will discuss them briefly here and throughout the remainder of the book I have included 2 checklists at the end of the chapter one for your business-related needs and one specifically for food related needs.

Paraphrasing from https://www.sba.gov/business-guide/10-steps-start-your-business/#step-1:

Conduct market research.

Market research will tell you if there's an opportunity to turn your idea into a successful food cart business. It's a way to gather information about potential guests, businesses and direct competitors already operating in your area. Use that information to find a competitive advantage for your business.

Write your business plan.

Your business plan is the foundation of your food service business. It's a roadmap for how to structure, run, and grow your that business. You'll use it to convince people that working with you — or investing in your company — is a smart choice.

TO DO Lists

Fund your business.

Your business plan will help you figure out how much money you'll need to start your business. If you don't have that amount on hand, you'll need to either raise or borrow the capital. Fortunately, there are more ways than ever to find the capital you need. I do not recommend going into debt. Street and event vending are weather driven. Facing loan payments after a wet, rainy summer is not fun. Debt influences your business decisions in a negative way, causing you to accept events you normally would not, "hoping" for a cash influx.

Pick your business location.

Your cart location is one of the most important decisions you'll make. Whether you're setting up at a single location, running a circuit or only working events, the choices you make could affect your taxes, legal requirements, and overall revenue.

Choose a business structure

The legal structure you choose for your business will impact your business registration requirements, how much you pay in taxes, and your personal liability. Generally, carts are Sole Proprietor or LLC. LLC are usually recommended by layman as the best solution for a business startup. On my blog I have a detailed explanation on the pitfalls of an LLC for a small one-person operation. https://moorebetterperformance.weebly.com/performance-blog/do-i-need-a-sole-proprietorship-or-llc-for-my-food-vending-business

Choose your business name.

It's not easy to pick the perfect name. You'll want one that reflects your brand, captures your spirit and food. You'll also want to make sure your business name isn't already being used by someone else.

Register your business.

Once you've picked the perfect business name, it's time to make it legal and protect your brand. If you're doing business under a name different than your own, you'll need to register with the federal government, and maybe your state government, too.

Get federal and state tax IDs.

You'll use your employer identification number (EIN) for important steps to start and grow your business, like opening a bank account and paying taxes. It's like a social security number for your business. Some — but not all — states require you to get a tax ID as well.

Apply for licenses and permits.

Keep your business running smoothly by staying legally compliant. The licenses and permits you need for your business will vary by industry, state, location, and other factors.

Open a business bank account.

A small business checking account can help you handle legal, tax, and day-to-day issues. The good news is it's easy to set one up if you have the right registrations and paperwork ready.

The graphics on the next two pages represent the generic SBA steps and the food service specific steps you must do to achieve your food dream at the level you envision. Several steps will overlap or seem redundant; however, they are vital to your business success. We will focus on the food related research and information you will need to be successful in the remaining chapters. As you are researching, and learning keep the SBA TO DO list handy and refer to it as you research. Much of your business plan can be filled out with information contained here or what you find on your searches. Using a note taking application like OneNote will assist you in organizing your information and makes the business plan part of your start up much less daunting. As always if you get stuck email me I'll help you write a good business plan for your area.

TO DO Lists

SBA TO DO List

 Conduct market **research.**

 Write your business **plan.**

 Fund your business.

 Pick your business **location.**

 Choose a business **structure**

 Choose your business **name.**

 Register your business.

 Get federal and state tax **IDs.**

 Apply for **licenses and permits.**

 Open a business **bank account.**

Putting the Cart Before the Dog

Food Service TO DO List

RESEARCH
Read your states food codes, local restrictions and the requirements for setting up a new business

MENU
Develop a menu based on what you are allowed sell in your state and what you will be proud to serve

SUPPLIERS
Find sources for quality food, paper & cleaning supplies as well as services such as a commissary

LOCATION
Steady locations to sell your food as well as special events to gain the most exposure and profits

EQUIPMENT
Shop for the best equipment you can afford. Practice & test while waiting for licenses

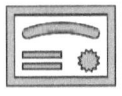
LICENSES
Apply for food licenses and other required permits. Get ready to open for business!

MENTOR
Confused? At any time, partner with an experienced mentor to quickly get operational and profitable!

RESEARCH

Begin with the end in mind. **Steven Covey**

Steven Covey teaches us to put first things first. Good advice. Often people jump at the salesman's pitch and have buyer's remorse later. Having dollar signs in their eyes they either fight through every step to success or give up at the first difficulty. Either way is a massive waste of time, resources and energy. Be smart, properly set your goal, develop a plan and then work the plan to achieve your goal. Short term you want a hot dog cart for whatever your personal reason may be. Long term you want financial security and peace of mind. Sound like an insurance salesman, don't I?

What is the first thing to do? Gather as much information as possible BEFORE spending a cent. Where do you start? Google is your friend! Research, copy and paste, bookmark and keep everything that strikes your fancy. You can weed out the useless later. Below are the starting points I recommend. These will give you the information you need to decide if purchasing a cart and working it is something you really want to do. Some people don't want to deal with all the government red tape. If that is you, it is

Putting the Cart Before the Dog

better to know now than after you are down $5000 on a new cart. Please note we **are not** ready to look at cart sites yet. They are designed to draw you in and sell you a cart. They will offer free "training", free business guides or offers to join our exclusive "Pro" blah, blah, blah. Don't spend a cent on "insider" secrets or "special members only pricing". We will get into the ins and outs of carts, work flow and purchasing yours later. Right now, you are still trying this business on for size. Guest service is not for everyone and neither is business ownership. As you read through this information ask yourself "Is this business worth the hassle to achieve my financial dream?" If you ever say "no" stop and search for what will make you happy as an occupation. I love restaurants and food service after decades it is second nature to me.

1. Google your town or city by name and add "starting a business". Look for checklists on what is needed, as well as, lists of office/department names and officials you will need to contact.
2. Google your state's department of revenue and search starting a business there.
3. Go to the IRS.gov web site and search for starting a business and follow its links.
4. While on each site write down department names and contact numbers on the form I have included here.
5. If you need clarification call someone and ask all the questions you have. We are gathering all the info we can BEFORE spending money.

The following is a screen shot of my search in Google. "Fort Walton Beach Florida" is, of course, my town preceded by "starting a business". Only go to state or county sites, the ads are designed to sell some service you don't need right now or maybe never. If you don't like Google use your preferred search engine.

RESEARCH

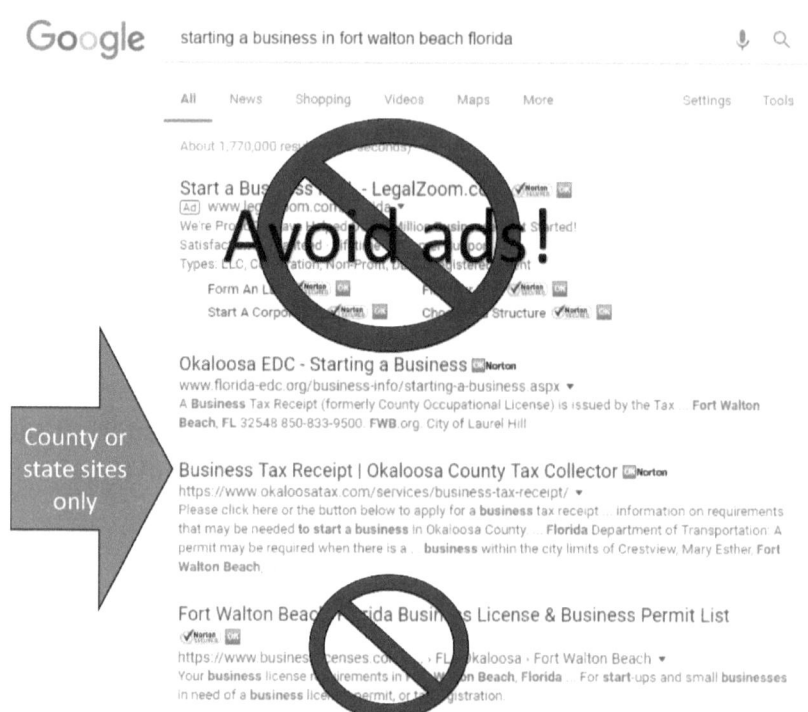

Now that you have working knowledge on starting a business in your state. It is time to turn your attention to the specifics of food vending in your area. Start locally because your area may have restrictions on street vending and you need to know those restrictions as soon as possible **before** buying your cart. Some cities allow vending but limit the number of permits issued or they limit the hours you are allowed to be opened. It is possible you will have a fight on your hands if the local commissions have been influenced by brick and mortar restaurant owners. Chains don't really care but small restaurant owners do. They are afraid of competition. You can win the fight, but it may take time and possibly money. If you are already struggling financially, find another more accommodating town to start your food vending career. The next township may be a better choice anyway. It could be as simple as vending just outside city limits on county land.

Putting the Cart Before the Dog

You will need some time to sift through all the information. The local governments and health departments will be the most confusing. Good news is you can set up an appointment to meet in person and discuss any questions you may have. Get information from the horse's mouth so to speak. Just get any rules and regulations in writing, so there will be no confusion later.

Google "starting a hot dog cart business" and add your "state". Again, ignore ads and look for state health department sites. Learn the differences in a HOT DOG VENDOR and a MFDV (mobile food dispensing vehicle) if your state has both.

Below is a screen shot of my results. As you will notice cart sellers come up BEFORE the information that we need to even be able to decide which cart and which options are legally required. We will have plenty of time later to check out the manufacturers.

RESEARCH

After the research for information, you probably have more questions than when you started. Most regulations are written by a lawyer and normal people don't read BS. Questions mean you want to learn and be good at food vending.

Time to make some calls and set appointments and talk to the officials in your location. They will, in most cases, be helpful because you are a potential source of revenue for the county or state.

Here are a few questions to get you started.

Local government:
1. Are there any restrictions for mobile food vendors?
2. What licenses/inspections will I need at the city/county level to operate my business? (occupation, fire, tax for example)
3. What taxes must I collect for the county and city?
4. Are there any reports I am required to file?

For the health department:
(Have an idea of your menu's food offerings. They don't care about your prices)

1. **I plan on selling xxx, xxx, and xxx would these be restricted on a Hot Dog vendor license?** List everything that you would prepare or cook. Make certain to ask specifically about a meat chili and real dairy cheese, both of these are restricted in some states. (Canned drinks or packaged foods like chips and candies won't matter) For example, in Florida a Hot Dog Vendor cannot sell a meat sauce or cook onions, but a MFDV can.
2. **How many sinks do I need?** If more than a hand wash sink is required does it need to be separated or divided from the others?
3. **What size fresh and waste water tanks do I need?**
4. **Where can I find the inspections for commissaries (or whatever your state calls it)?** How are commissaries noted on inspections? Some departments will tell who offers commissary services and some won't because they aren't allowed to "endorse" one over the other. Inspections on the other hand are public record and you are justified in seeing

those inspections to make an informed decision. You do not want your cart associated with a commissary that was closed (even for a few hours) due to failing an inspection.

5. **Are you the only state agency that approves mobile vendors and commissaries?** In Florida, we have 3 different agencies that regulate food establishments. Your license must match the commissary's license and you will need to send the plan reviews and licensing fees to the correct agency.
6. **Where am I required to store my cart when not in use?** Some areas require it be kept at the commissary and you cannot store it at home.
7. **I plan to offer catering in addition to my normal business will this require a different type of license or different inspections?**

For the state revenue department:
1. **Requirements to open a business.**
2. **Reporting and payment schedule.** (Think you are a nobody? miss a tax payment you'll be somebody quickly!)
3. **Fictitious Name requirements** (if needed)
4. **Any state or federal funding programs or grants for my area or business?** (You never know!)

Add anything else you are not sure about. It is better to ask too many questions than not enough.

Use the sheet on the following page as you do your research. Write down all the important numbers. I keep this sheet in a book on my cart or in my van. If I get some inspector or official visit I know who I contacted and who I talked to about everything concerning my business. This can diffuse a difficult situation quickly and get all parties on the same page. If you expand to multiple carts each cart should have important numbers available just in case, you are not around.

At this point in your research you will not have either the insurance or accountant information. Add those later as you get closer to opening your business.

RESEARCH

Contacts and Phone Numbers

Fill out this page and keep these numbers handy.

Chamber of Commerce where you will vend

- Name of contact _____
- Phone Number _____

City government offices where you will vend

- Department name _____
- Name of contact _____
- Phone Number _____

County tax collector where you will vend

- Department name _____
- Name of contact _____
- Phone Number _____

State Department of Revenue where you will vend

- Department name _____
- Name of contact _____
- Phone Number _____

County Health Department or similar agency

- County level office _____
- Name of contact _____
- Phone Number _____

Liability Insurance

- Company _____
- Agent Name _____
- Phone Number _____
- Policy Number _____

Accountant/Tax Preparer

- Name _____
- Phone number _____

Final Word on Restrictive Laws

Local regulations are the third biggest challenge outside of finding a commissary (second) and location(first). You may find you live in an area that restricts street vending via a certain number of permits allowed or even completely prohibits such businesses. You can choose to fight, as many of the laws are written poorly and can be overturned easily. Or you can find another town for your business. That is up to you. The courts today are interpreting the word "liberty" in the Constitution and applying it to commerce as well as personal freedom. Thus, street vendors cannot be prevented from operating their business. BUT, and that is a big BUT, interpretations could change. States have always been given broad local police (as in writing laws) powers. A well written and non-discriminatory law will not be overturned in court as the court cannot "bench legislate" and will bow to states' police power rights. Luckily for us most laws that try to prevent street vending are written specifically to discriminate against a business that nearly the entire US recognizes as legitimate, dating back to the 1600s. (Street vending not hot dog carts. LOL)

If you are told by an official street vending is not allowed, politely ask to see the regulation that says so. Get a copy if possible. Go to http://ij.org for more information how to fight unfair laws. If nothing else read this report by the lawyers at IJ.org http://ij.org/wp-content/uploads/2016/10/Open-For-Business-web.pdf

This is completely different than an official giving you incorrect information. Often rules are subject to interpretation and this creates gray areas and enforcement inconsistencies. This is where you should definitely fight, and you will win. Check out Facebook in your area for hot dog vendors. If one exists, then you can exist. If your setup mirrors their setup you cannot be stopped from operating. If there are no street vendors in your area, you might be facing an uphill regulatory battle. Laws can be changed or struck down. Just remember you will sleep better at night if you are <u>legally</u> setup, following all rules, regulations and paying your taxes on time. Best of all if you are making 59% profit your sleep will be quite peaceful.

RESEARCH

By this point you have a few hours invested in research and should have a general idea about cost before making the big purchases of cart and supplies. One last point I want to stress. Cart manufacturers have a ton of info on their sites and <u>generally,</u> it is good information. The caveat is somewhere on the site in its T&C of use will be a disclaimer about you doing the due diligence before purchasing a cart. Smart advice. Only use a cart manufacturer site to purchase a cart, period. Remember, you are the one on the front line dealing with vendors, inspectors, city officials and, most importantly, guests. The sales person or web designer at the hot dog cart manufacturer is not. You want to be able to understand your areas regulations and operate within those regulations.

As I mentioned before there are over 3000 different versions of Food Codes in the US. If you are planning your business to operate from a single city or county all you need to know is one. If your dream includes traveling a circuit in different counties or states, you will need to know those laws as well. State laws vary enough that you may not be able to take a cart on a state to state road trip. For example, in Georgia a hot dog cart must have 4 sinks where as in Florida a Hot Dog vendor license allows only 1 sink. Both states require the license number be prominently displayed on the cart. Each regulation can be met by a vendor with the same cart if you understand the codes and come up with acceptable solutions for both states. Think long term about where you want to vend and how you plan on growing.

Another part of Steven Covey's book, 7 Habits of Highly Effective People is: *Begin with the end in mind.* Most people get so excited to start that they forget to plan the end. Not the end of the business but what you are really getting into the business to accomplish. Retirement, vacations, new home, building a company to leave to your kids, whatever your reason to start vending, remember it is only the vehicle transporting you your end goal.

If you are confused just email me and we will go over your state laws together. I'll help you, that is what I live for.

MENU

It all comes back to the basics. Serve customers the best-tasting food at a good value in a clean, comfortable restaurant, and they'll keep coming back. **Dave Thomas, founder Wendy's International**

Now that you know the legal requirements and the associated permit and license costs it is time to work on portions and procedures for your food. You can always refine them later. This is to determine what equipment you will need on the cart. I will stick with the basics of hot dogs, but realize you are only limited by your health department license and your cooking ability.

First, how are you going to cook the hot dogs? This is a debate that rages on and while it can be dictated by regional tastes, it is up to you and your tastes. Remember McDonalds, Burger King and Wendy's can all be on the same street and do equally well. Each has a distinct cooking method, generally people favor service and taste over cooking method when they are pressed for time. Lunch break from work, for example. McDonalds places speed as the number one driving choice factor, then value and flavor. (http://www.nrn.com/technology/mcdonald-s-focus-speed) Just because everyone else boils, you aren't locked into doing the same.

MENU

What tastes good to you, what will you be proud to serve and what will you be able to handle at the busy times should dictate how you cook. I, personally, like grilled the best but it can be challenging to keep up with this cooking method. It does create smoke and aromas that are free advertising for your business. Who can smell that smoky goodness and not get hungry?

Method	Heat Source	Fuel	Pros	Cons
Grilled	open fire	charcoal, propane, wood	smoke attracts guests	wind blow smoke in your or guests face
			distinct flavor profile and appearance	very easy to over cook/burn
			evokes memories of cookouts, family reunions, etc.	Guest can make this at home
			easy to "stage" cook	
Steamed	water heated by flame	generally propane	evokes memories of fairs and boardwalks	difficult to determine interal temperature from appearance
			"pure" hot dog flavor	over time will shrivel or explode
			can flavor steam to create unique product	flavor can be too subtle to notice
			Cooking limited by pan size / product exposure to steam	slow recovery time if you run out
Boiled	submerged in boiling water	generally propane	Many street vendors use this method	you are now one of many
			Flavor the water to create a unique signature product	hard to keep a consistent flavor
			Easiest method to cook in volume	recovery can be an issue but is quicker than steaming methods
			easiest method to hold hot	easy to dilute the hot dog flavor

    Of course, you can combine the methods to produce your signature style. For example, you can boil the dogs from frozen in beef stock and spices in about 6 to 7 minutes. Then turn down the heat to hold them above 135 degrees (140 degrees in states using older FDA models and you will learn this in food safety classes.) When the dog is ordered, you can then put it on the grill to add the classic grill marks and caramelization. Keeping the grill hot enough to do this in a few seconds is the first key to quick SOS (speed of service). Also, prestaging as guests enter your serving line makes this fairly easy. This method, then, becomes your signature method for your product, a point of difference between you and all the other vendors. The flavor is now distinct, the look is appealing, and this creates the taste experience that will bring the guest back more often. The most damaging thing you can do is take "shortcuts" when it is busy, or you fall behind in service. If I get a tasty dog with beautiful grill marks today and bring my family back tomorrow to share my experience and you have gotten in "the weeds" and don't finish the dog on the grill to save time, then I am now disappointed and may not come back, **ever**. Being a restaurant professional, I begin to question what other things you will short cut when under pressure. Perhaps you will serve me something undercooked, or short cut sanitation and proper food handling to get cleaned up quicker. On a side note, I watched a "Q&A" live stream produced by a cart seller that **promoted being inconsistent and offered wrong food safety information**. First, they wrongly stated hot holding is a minimum **143 degrees** (It is 135 or 140 depending on which version of the FDA code is used). Second, they stated when business is slow they will put the dogs on the grill to make it "sexy" and create that enticing aroma but when busy it goes straight on the bun. What?!? I wonder if the same shortcut mentality is used when he manufactures his carts?

  Hot dog vendors call the boiling method, "dirty water dogs", the water becomes murky as you cook. Fats break down, seasonings and coloring leach out, basically, you are creating a hot dog "stock" much like creating beef stock using tough cuts of meat, bones, water and seasonings. Since the goal is heating the dog rather than creating stock, you must add back a flavor to the water that will infuse the dogs. That is why I mentioned beef stock. You can use anything to flavor the water. Flat beer, onions, garlic, bouillon cubes, chicken stock, seasoning mixes, beef au jus or anything else that will add a unique memorable flavor. One last thing on boiling, while it is known as "dirty water" don't get used to calling it that. Would you want to hear "dirty water" coming from a cook's mouth referencing food you are about to eat? There is a certain decorum expected from food service. By all means have fun but also be tasteful. (get it!!)

Once you develop a procedure stick to it. You will get faster and faster and make fewer mistakes if you make yourself **do it right every time**. Restaurant chains often run competitions to keep skills honed and to demonstrate that following procedures correctly can still be fast. Burger King runs contests where you compete in making a fully dressed, correctly portioned Whopper as fast as possible. (Here is a write up from 2013 http://www.mywnynews.com/arcade_warsaw/people/spotlight_on/article_cf4dcf18-2c5d-11e3-a512-001a4bcf887a.html) The product is then weighed and inspected for correct portions. The winner must be fast but also accurate. FYI, the winner is around the 10 to 11 second mark, making a Whopper with mayo covering the entire crown surface, 1oz. shredded lettuce covering the mayo and two tomatoes laid side by side, the burger placed on the heel gets 3 rings of ketchup, 2 rings of mustard, 4 pickles placed separately, 4 onion rings also placed separately. The crown is then placed on the heel section using the tomatoes to hold the lettuce in place and wrapped using the "Christmas package" style wrap. 11 seconds! BK also runs a contest on the Original Chicken preparation and that winner is 8 seconds. Want to fail??? Be inconsistent and don't practice it works every time. Remember the "secret"? Training and practice are the first two elements!

You now know how to cook your hot dogs; the next important thing is what brand? The area you are in will dictate this. Even neighborhoods might have different favorites. All beef, all meat, chicken, turkey, sausage which to choose? Your questions to the health department may help here. If you are a hot dog only vendor meaning your license only allows precooked frankfurters you are limited to just that. In essence, you are heating rather than cooking the hot dogs. No raw meats on your cart! You should also know if dairy cheese is allowed. If it is banned as well as a meat based chili you could make a veggie chili sauce and use processed cheese in a can like Cheese Wiz. Whatever you are allowed to sell, make a trip to the closest grocery store to your main location. Go to the hot dog section and see which brand has the largest area for display. That most likely is the favorite brand of the neighborhood. Now go to other groceries nearby and see if that observation holds true. Walmart is not the best indicator of best-selling brand. Walmart and national/regional grocery chains allocate cooler shelf space as directed by corporate offices and contractual obligations with the brands. Nationwide Oscar Mayer is most popular, and this is reflected by the amount of space for its hot dogs. Locally, however, it may not be the best seller <u>but</u> will have the largest shelf allotment. Another factor to check is the expiration dates and manufacture run of the front packages vs the ones in the back. Come back after a busy weekend and recheck the dates. You will know what sold and what didn't. Once you determine the brand you want to sell. You want to see if the brand has a vendor program, here you could get discounted branded items like banners, hats or marketing materials. If you are selling a name brand, brag about it!

You could also sell a no name, all meat dog. Sam's Club has an 8 to 1 (restaurant jargon for 8 dogs to 1 pound) dog for $14.98 a case in my area (as of 4/3/2017) that is 18.73 cents apiece. I sell these as my 2 dog, chip and drink combo for $8.00. I also carry Nathan's ¼ lbs. dog because I love the taste.

After the meat decision, time to decide on bread carrier. Will you use a split top, side cut or something else? Side cut is most easily available. Heating the bun is a must. Steaming is most popular, but toasting is better. However, toasting on a cart is extremely difficult. Consistency is the main issue, as well as, the

MENU

process is slow or requires electricity for a fast restaurant quality toaster. Putting buns on a grill to get exterior grill marks is not always the best idea. Bread caramelizes differently than meats. The taste is profoundly more bitter. Think about a burnt piece of toast at home, what you do to fix it. Scrape off the dark caramelized parts. So why attempt to do this on a cart? Some "guru" recommends it!

Condiments are next. What will you include on your hot dogs? Who will apply what? Are you dressing the dog completely or will the guest receive a plain dog to dress how they want or will you do part and the guest do part? Fastest is a plain dog and a condiment bar set up away from your service area. It is also the costliest and you will need to restock the bar often. Slowest is you doing all the dressing, handling all the requests for extras but this is most cost effective. Remember that Original Chicken sandwich from BK dressed in 8 seconds? For BK, that is a 6" sub roll with mayonnaise on the crown and heel covering end to end, 1 oz. of lettuce covering the mayo on the crown, chicken patty on the heel, covered with crown and wrapped, all in 8 seconds. In general terms, a hot dog vendor applies condiments to the hot dog itself (a Chicago Dog is a notable exception) and not the bun following this pattern of most fluid condiment (mustard, ketchup) to semi-fluid (meat sauce, liquid cheese) to chunky (diced onions, relish) ending with dry (seasonings and spices).

If you can match the speed of a BK employee making an Original Chicken Sandwich, you would make exactly 7.5 hot dogs per minute. The guest will take much longer to order than it will take you to prepare, so you are looking at most, a sale of $7.00 (2 dogs, chips & drink combo) **every minute** which will translate into $1260 a day with a steady flow of guests for three hours. Remember that number? This is more than it will take to reach over $100,000 **profit** before income taxes!

Putting the Cart Before the Dog

I put everything on myself. But I also have made 10's of thousands of burgers and hot dogs over the years so I am really, really, fast and I am a bit of a control freak when it comes to costs. When I allow guests to dress the entire dog my food/paper cost closer to 38-39%, when I do all it is 28-30%. Another way to look at it if you pay someone to work with you, only during service, at $15.00 an hour and can completely dress the dog for the 28% cost you will spend $45.00 in labor a day of your $1260 sales goal. (I have hired school bus drivers to do this as 11am to 2pm is perfect for them) If you allow the guest to dress it and you work alone the cost is, on the low side, $100.80. Plus, you are working harder to keep the condiment bar filled and cleaned during service. Last thing on condiments. How many have to be held hot? Chili, liquid cheese, sauerkraut, grilled onions, onions & peppers, bacon. You get the idea. Each of these dictate your cart steam table specs and pan sizes.

Use portion control every chance you get. Use a 1oz. ladle for chili, use old fashioned measuring cups for grated cheese. When I worked at Wendy's in the early 90's they used measuring cups for all prep work AND sandwich assembly. Cheese, bacon bits, diced tomatoes all were measured every day, every time. We made 100's of side and Caesar salads a day and never used "sight" as a measurement. Besides cost control you get consistency. Every dog you sell should look like the last.

Go to your local fast food restaurant and get several ketchup, mayo and mustard packets. Carefully cut the corner of each packet and dress a plain dog. Does the amount look correct? Does it need more? If so add one full packet and judge again. Once you have determined the right look, taste it. Does one flavor dominate? Once you are satisfied with the look and flavor, check the packets for portion. Now you know how much to put on your dogs and can now figure the cost per serving. This is something you will have to depend on sight and practice to get control on the portions (For condiments in squeeze bottles). Many stands use pumps to dispense liquid condiments. These are "OK" dispensers, they are usually made out of plastic and are terribly fragile and inconsistent. The plastic will stain with the color of the condiment and take on that flavor. These pumps are nearly impossible to clean properly, retain water after cleaning and need replaced often. A stainless-steel pump is better but has several parts that are easy to lose (O-rings, ball bearings and cotter pins) and have to be taken completely apart and cleaned every day.

     I use refillable bottles. The so called "pros" recommended "first in first out bottles". Well... they have design problems. On the surface, they seem brilliant. A bottle that has two removable caps. One end has the portion control serving opening and the other end has a solid screw on lid. This is the end where you would add new product and the other end is to dispense the "old" product. Burger King recommends these and uses them for several different sauces of varying thickness. The theory is you can store them dispensing side down, grab and dispense what is needed without that first "shake" to get the product to the end of the bottle. Then return the bottle user end down till the next time. Problems in the practical use are: the dispensing end tends to leak after just a little use, usually a couple of meal periods, these lids have a thin flexible diaphragm that wears out and the entire lid must be replaced. The diaphragm eventually just stops sealing, and leaks, forcing the operator to turn the bottle upside down. Also, there are different sized dispensing lid openings for thicker and thinner condiments, so you have to have more bottles with different matching lids. The required "squeeze" to get the condiment flowing varies from lid to lid based on the wear of the diaphragm, making one strength of squeeze dispense way too much product or you get a sudden dispensing blob. Also, the temptation is to consistently refill which means you never break the bacteria cycle. Think about it for a second, thinking a liquid doesn't "mix" when you pick it up and move it around is crazy. You really aren't FIFOing anything.

The bottles I use are old fashioned bottles with one opening and a pointed dispenser. I cut the opening to different sizes for the mustard, ketchup and mayo. I then have a certain "bead" size for each that when applied correctly tastes good without overwhelming the dog. McDonalds uses a gun similar to a caulking gun for Big Mac sauce and Tartar sauce. One squeeze one portion. They also have mustard and ketchup dispensers that work similarly. One squeeze one portion. The mustard dispenser has only two openings and the ketchup dispenser have three. That is why your cheese burger often has little dots of condiments.

I saw a "pro" training video bragging about someone using a caulking gun and how brilliant that was. My wife and I looked at each other and laughed (both served time... I mean worked at McDonalds decades apart) knowing Mickey D's been using that since, well, forever.

On page 36 is a spreadsheet I use to cost my menu. I list every possible topping as being included on my hot dogs. This way I know the highest point my food cost should reach per item. Don't get wrapped up in the details of brands I chose. Change what you want. It is your business. This is to give you a general idea of what to sell and how to price it based on real costs as of 4/19/2017. Every product will be priced as premade, rather than prepped at the commissary. Meaning I priced Cole Slaw in a tub rather than buying cabbage, carrots and a mix to prep it. Prepping your own Cole Slaw, relish, chili, sauerkraut or any other topping will save you money. But does add prep time to your commissary visits. Some commissaries charge by the hour. You must decide which way is more cost effective for you while maintaining taste and quality.

MENU

portion size	Ingredient	portions	cost	cost/portion	8 to 1		4 to 1	
each	hot dogs 8/1 sz	80	$ 14.98	$ 0.19	1	$ 0.19		$ -
each	hot dogs 1/4 lbs	160	$ 114.08	$ 0.71		$ -	1	$ 0.71
						$ -		$ -
3 oz	Nacho Cheese	48	$ 6.98	$ 0.15		$ -		$ -
1 oz	Cheddar Cheese	80	$ 12.98	$ 0.16	1	$ 0.16	1	$ 0.16
each	buns	16	$ 2.28	$ 0.14	1	$ 0.14	1	$ 0.14
3/4 oz	Mayonnaise	171	$ 6.98	$ 0.04	1	$ 0.04	1	$ 0.04
1/2 oz	relish bulk	256	$ 5.34	$ 0.02	1	$ 0.02	1	$ 0.02
.67 oz	mustard bulk	156	$ 4.28	$ 0.03	1	$ 0.03	1	$ 0.03
3/4 oz	ketchup bulk	152	$ 3.83	$ 0.03	1	$ 0.03	1	$ 0.03
1 oz	chili	90	$ 6.03	$ 0.07	1	$ 0.07	1	$ 0.07
1/2 oz (4-5)	Jalapenos	256	$ 6.68	$ 0.03	1	$ 0.03	1	$ 0.03
1/2 oz	onions	300	$ 4.98	$ 0.02	1	$ 0.02	1	$ 0.02
3/4 oz	cole slaw	106	$ 4.98	$ 0.05	1	$ 0.05	1	$ 0.05
each	chips	50	$ 12.72	$ 0.25		$ -		$ -
each	Fritos	50	$ 12.72	$ 0.25		$ -		$ -
each	soda (Coke 12oz)	35	$ 10.98	$ 0.31		$ -		$ -
each	water (16 oz)	40	$ 4.98	$ 0.12		$ -		$ -
each	cookies	42	$ 12.58	$ 0.30		$ -		$ -
each	hot dog tray	750	$ 7.96	$ 0.01	1	$ 0.01	1	$ 0.01
each	foil sleeves	1000	$ 55.96	$ 0.06	1	$ 0.06	1	$ 0.06
each	6# carryout bag	500	$ 22.94	$ 0.05	0.3	$ 0.01	0.25	$ 0.01
each	sm clamshell	250	$ 13.57	$ 0.05		$ -		$ -
each	napkins (tall)	4500	$ 18.92	$ 0.00	3	$ 0.01	3	$ 0.01
each	food gloves	2000	$ 10.78	$ 0.01	1	$ 0.01	1	$ 0.01
					total cost	$ 0.86		$ 1.38

	Combo Food Cost					
	HD/chip/drink	2 HD/chip/drink		HD/chip/drink	2 sand/chp/drnk	
8 to 1 Menu price	$5.00	$8.00	4 to 1 Menu price	$7.00	$11.00	
	30.48%	30.46%		29.70%	32.24%	

Read over the spreadsheet carefully. You will note I cost 3 napkins per dog, as well as, 1 glove. The reason I list a single glove is I know most of my sales with either be a combo or just drinks. I cost a single glove in <u>everything</u> I sell. This accounts for more gloves than I actually use thus my glove budget is well funded. I also cost napkins for sodas and chips too. Notice I use foil bags rather than Styrofoam hot dog clamshells. While clamshells are slightly faster to use, and require one less paper item (trays), the drawback is the amount of space they occupy, both in storage and also in the TRASH. If you have a seating area near by these containers will eat up your trash cans quickly.

For marketing, I picture my one Dog (8 to 1) Combo dressed only with Chili, Cheddar Cheese, Onions and Mustard along with a bag of chips and a bottled water. This picture has a star burst price of $5.00. It is on a folding 4x3 foot sign in front of my cart. This is the only picture in use. The price point draws people in, once they commit to eating with me, I must trade them up. This picture also focuses what is ordered. Guest usually says something like "give me that combo you advertise." I respond with, "dressed just like the picture?" 80% say "yes" or "yes but leave off the onions". My final question is "I've got a 2-dog combo for only $8, would you like that?" Generally, the guest will then scan my written menu and notice that combination will save $2.00 off the individual pricing or upgrade themselves to the 4 to 1 Dog Combo. Either way I have increased sales and profitability.

Dressed as pictured the food/paper cost is 27.09% for a single dog combo and 26.23% for the 2-dog combo. 4 guests out of 10 order this exact combo and another 3 of 10 exchange the water for soda!

A point of difference for me is what I cook and prep at my commissary. A commissary should offer not only cleaning and storage but cooking equipment and a prep area as well. Most states require daily visits for a commissary. In reality, you may need TWO visits. If you are required to store your food and cart there, obviously two visits are needed. One to pick up and one to clean and drop off. I pick up inventory and only prep fresh onions in the morning. I am in the commissary less than 20 minutes. In the afternoon, I prep my next day's food. I make my own Cole Slaw (I'm a bit of snob about Cole Slaw) and chili. I make one of each on different days. The chili I let simmer while I am washing the pans and cart. I am always thinking how can I do this or that faster or more efficiently. I am always looking to improve. You should too.

MENU

Here is a copy of my limited menu (page 39) I use when I go to certain locations, like festivals or fire work displays. (I have a bigger menu I use for other venues and requires I have a helper) Just remember if your state only allows a hot dog vendor to deal in precooked frankfurters, you must comply. In Florida, we have TWO different vendor types, Hot Dog and Mobile Food Dispensing Units, MFDV are allowed a broader menu and that is what my license covers. Doesn't mean I <u>have</u> to sell more than hot dogs, but it does allow me to cook chili or caramelize onions and add that to my dogs.

If you live in an area that expect certain toppings, you should carry them. Price the dog accordingly. If you can sell the basics while hitting your sales goal, then do that. At minimum, for instance, when I sell at Little League games I cut down to one dog type, mustard, ketchup, onions, relish, couple of chip types, regular & diet Coke, Sprite, water but I also add Gatorade, popcorn and packaged peanuts. This has that *stadium* feel to it. But when I sell near the beach the menu changes to fit that environment. I also have a different menu when I sell at fairs. My license allows it, so I use it. I can set you up a personalized menu analysis on a spreadsheet just email me and ask.

My menu shows a theme based on the business name "Pirate Dogs". We will talk about this later in branding and marketing. For now, look at the combo section. I sell mostly in combo form. At the beach, families eat up (literally) that combo with extra drinks. That is a 28.60% food cost (mix in water for soda and it is lower). Compared to buying it all separately the guest saves $7.50 a great perceived value. Remember, my prices are high, influenced by the tourists and beach. You may find your area requires lower pricing. For example, a $7.00 2 dog combo is quite common in much of the US. That leaves a 32.85% food/paper cost for a fully dressed combo. Still profitable. The commonly ordered toppings yield a 29.97% cost. Plenty of profit still left at that price point!

Putting the Cart Before the Dog

		Galley Mains		
Deck Hand Dog	Regular Beef Hot Dog on a Steamed Bun with Pirate Chili, Grated Sharp Cheddar, Diced Onions and Yellow Mustard	**$4.00**		
		with Chips or Cole Slaw & Soda or Water	$	5.00
		with Planks & Soda or Water	$	7.00
		Add a 2nd Deck Hand to a Combo	$	3.00
Quarter Master Dog	Nathan's Famous 1/4 lbs. Hot Dog on a Steamed Bun with Pirate Chili, Grated Sharp Cheddar, Diced Onions and Yellow Mustard	**$5.00**		
		with Chips or Cole Slaw & Soda or Water	$	6.00
		with Planks & Soda or Water	$	8.00
		Add a 2nd Quarter Master to a Combo	$	4.00
		Sides		
Walkin' Da Planks	Frito Brand corn chips covered in Texas style chili, and grated cheddar cheese	**$3.50**		
Cole Slaw	Sweet like me Granny used to make	**$1.00**		
Chips	Lays Brand	**$1.00**		
		Something Sweet		
Cookies	Famous Amos Chocolate Chip	**$1.00**		
		This ain't Rum		
Soda	Coke, Diet Coke, Sprite, Dr Pepper and Mountain Dew	**$1.50**		
Water	Zephyrhills Spring Water	**$1.50**		
Gatorade	Various	**$2.50**		

Pirate Dogs

    I have included a list of regional favorites (page 52) for you to get some inspiration. If you live in one of these areas, you may have to carry these toppings as they are the guest's expectation. Every burger chain has Mayo, Ketchup, Pickles, Onions, Tomatoes, Lettuce and Mustard. Every chain recognizes the need to offer local or regional favorites. That is why when you travel away from your area your favorite chain may not carry what your home store may carry. You'll need at the very least Ketchup, Mustard, Chili (if you are allowed), Diced Raw Onions, Relish and Cheese plus whatever your area expects. Other condiments to consider: mayo (since I make Cole Slaw this gives me another outlet to turn over product), brown mustards, hot sauces, sauerkraut, red onion sauce (New York style), hot liquid cheese, pickle spears, sport peppers, jalapeno peppers, candied jalapenos, pickle relish, onion relish, specialty salts, ground seasonings, flavored ketchups and anything else your feel will set you apart as the best hot dog vendor.

Pricing Your Menu

Price is what you pay. Value is what you get. **Warren Buffett**

Pricing your menu properly can be scary especially if you have never sold anything. Assigning value is difficult for some people. Make prices too low and you may be quite busy, but have little to show for it. Go too high and no one stops to eat. In pricing, you have to be Goldilocks, finding that "just right" balance of price vs value.

Value goes beyond high quality products on your menu. Value is perceived in delivery of said menu. Clean cart, fantastic service, witty interaction with your guests, location convenience all play a part in adding value to your product.

How many times have you groaned at the price of toilet paper at a convenience store only to buy it anyway because it saved you time? Your location provides a food choice for your guests saving them time, gasoline and trouble.

As I have noted I work on the beach a lot, so my pricing is higher than other areas in the USA. I once set up 5 days a week at a very remote subdivision being built by a developer that had 100 to 150 workers. It was located an hour inland and 20 minutes from the nearest town. The closest and only food was pizza, with limited toppings, made in a very old dirty Exxon station with 2 gas pumps. (The kind that dinged every gallon!) I set up shop in the middle of the subdivision using my higher beach pricing without a problem. By the end of construction nearly the entire group of workers was eating with me. This was one of those situations where I actually did work about 3 hours a day from prep to service to cleanup. Because the entire site shut down at once for lunch I had to have help handing the crowd, so they had enough time to eat. Location convenience does add value justifying higher prices.

Pricing your menu is strictly a function of profitability. Your menu most likely will be your only revenue stream, as such you must understand your P&L completely. Earlier I showed you a statement for sales of $100,000 with all the break down in costs. Nearly all the guru "pros" simplify the P&L to Income Less Expenses Equal Profit. Then don't bother to explain details or they lump everything associated with the menu, clean up, cooking and maintenance and call that COGS (cost of goods). This is where their naiveté in the food business becomes apparent. According to Investopedia COGS is:

> The exact costs included in the COGS calculation will differ from one type of business to another. The cost of goods attributed to a company's products are expensed as the company sells these goods. There are several ways to calculate COGS but one of the more basic ways is to start with the beginning inventory for the period and add the total amount of purchases made during the period, and then deducting the ending inventory. This calculation gives the total amount of inventory or, more specifically, the cost of this inventory, sold by the company during the period. Therefore, if a company starts with $10 million in inventory, makes $2 million in purchases and ends the period with $9 million in inventory, the company's cost of goods for the period would be $3 million ($10 million + $2 million - $9 million).

Did you notice "ends the period with $9 million in inventory"? That means a physical count of materials was made by someone. Also notice COGS does not include the utilities (propane for us) or maintenance materials for equipment (paper towels, soap, etc.). These categories are the cost of doing business **not** the cost of goods. Two entirely different things.

In all the different concepts, I have worked, not one refers to COGS (except Quiznos and they do that because the vast majority of franchisees are people with exactly zero restaurant experience). This number is too generalized and impossible to look at and then analyze. Restaurants breakdown the overall cost of goods in to bite sized (food pun!) bits of information that, at a glance, will reveal problem areas. At Burger King, for example, we had food, paper, condiments, shortening and supplies each with a budget target. (Food was even broken farther down by Burgers, Chicken, Bread, Cheese etc.) You are thinking how does food differ from condiments aren't you? In BK's case, food is everything an employee would portion, prep or prepare for a guest, this also included sodas and prepacked drinks. Condiments are packet items like ketchup, mustard, jelly, dipping sauces. Shortening was, of course, for the fryers. Paper was anything used for food delivery to a guest and supplies included cleaners, paper towels, scrubbing pads and the like.

If you are cruising along hitting 59% profit consistently and then suddenly it drops to 57% do you panic? Well if you have been grouping and separating costs you will see in seconds which areas are out of line. At that point, you can analyze only a few items and fix the problem going forward instead of shrugging your shoulders and going "I don't know" in a 6-year old's voice.

Since a cart menu is very limited I only use a few categories on my P&L. I lump food and paper together, this being anything that I handle that goes to the guest or that the guest has access to like napkins. I do a daily inventory and use this information to restock my food, paper and other supplies. When the month ends I take this inventory and figure a dollar amount for on-hand inventory.

Other categories include cleaning supplies, propane, gasoline, ice (I have an ice machine, so I don't purchase ice but if needed I include it in food simply because if I am open the ice melts and thus becomes waste.) and of course rents, fees, phone bills, etc.

Alright, boring P&L explanation out of the way. Now on to pricing. As I mentioned before when I price my food I include everything that a guest could possibly want on the hot dog. Then I look at different price points and ask, "would I pay that amount and is that price comparable to the competition?" Remember you don't have to be cheaper to be perceived as better. Here is my 8 to 1 hot

Ingredient & link	cost/portion	recipe		Food/paper $		Price Points		F/P %
hot dogs 8/1 sz	$ 0.19	1	$ 0.19	$	0.86	$	1.00	86.13%
Cheddar Cheese	$ 0.16	1	$ 0.16			$	1.50	57.42%
buns	$ 0.14	1	$ 0.14			$	2.00	43.07%
Mayonnaise	$ 0.04	1	$ 0.04			$	2.50	34.45%
relish bulk	$ 0.02	1	$ 0.02			$	3.00	28.71%
mustard bulk	$ 0.03	1	$ 0.03			$	3.50	24.61%
ketchup bulk	$ 0.03	1	$ 0.03			$	4.00	21.53%
chili	$ 0.07	1	$ 0.07			$	4.50	19.14%
Jalapenos	$ 0.03	1	$ 0.03			$	5.00	17.23%
onions	$ 0.02	1	$ 0.02			$	5.50	15.66%
cole slaw	$ 0.05	1	$ 0.05					
hot dog tray	$ 0.01	1	$ 0.01	Goal F/P %				
foil sleeves	$ 0.06	1	$ 0.06		32%	$	2.69	
6# carryout bag	$ 0.05	0.3	$ 0.01					
napkins (tall)	$ 0.00	3	$ 0.01					
food gloves	$ 0.01	1	$ 0.01					
		total cost	$ 0.86					

dog analysis:

You can see the different possible food cost percentages for each price point, as well as, the established goal percent. I can make you a spreadsheet to assist you in figuring your costs using your locations data or you can modify mine. I will leave a link to all

MENU

spreadsheets at the end of the last chapter. Oh yeah, for free, no email, no nothing!

In our earlier discussion on hot dogs I only touched on the different types of meat used to produce hot dogs. I wanted you to shop based on local popularity and personal taste. Now is time to decide whether an all-beef dog (only made with beef products) is the product you want to sell. Some areas of the country expect a brand like Vienna, while others only want all-beef and still others like all-meat (made with various animals and otherwise not normally consumed meat cuts). Or you could specialize in all-turkey, all-chicken or even veggie. Whatever will sell in your area, let customers dictate your menu and you will succeed.

One thing restaurant chains are notorious for doing is allowing trends and fads to influence what they add to menus. For example, while at Burger King I witnessed a ton of products added over the years and without fail they were dropped being a colossal waste of inventory, time and often new equipment. Often the managers would protest the new products and the complaints fell on deaf ears on the corporate side. Remember when in a campaign of "take away the no vote" started at BK a few years ago? The idea was to eliminate the person in group that would say "no" to a restaurant choice because that restaurant didn't sell a particular item. The mantra of "let's sell everything" began with adding tacos (frozen, deep fried to order and a SOS nightmare), baked potatoes, chili (made in the microwave with a ridiculous short hold time), English Muffin and Bagel breakfast sandwiches (so that was FOUR bread carriers at breakfast) and warm chicken added to salads. So, the attack was on Taco Bell, Wendy's and McDonalds. Now how many of those items are on the menu today? That would be zero (English Muffins come and go). Customer always dictate menu.

Now, with cart either ordered or in your driveway it is time to finalize your business and get ready for the first customer. How to cook, how to hold, how to dress and how to serve. What are the toppings, portions and what to charge? Time to research again. Search the web with "hot dog cart" and your city. Look for businesses that are up and running. Facebook is another place to search. My state has a 'verify a license' site, searchable by county and license type that shows all the hot dog carts and MFDVs. From there I can search the name and find menus, pictures of setups and locations. This will give you an idea of the prices your area will support. I would also visit the ones that are similar in setup, buy some food and strike up a conversation. Some vendors will be helpful, others are afraid of competition. At least you will have an idea of price, taste and personality of the competition.

  I stick with what I am proud to sell and don't mind eating mistakes. If you can afford a taste test, practice dry run by all means do it. Invite friends, family and neighbors, set up your cart or use your outdoor grill and let them taste small plain samples to make your final dog determination. Then prep the remaining full dogs as they would order from you. Practice, practice and more practice will increase your speed. When you are setup at a closed event where all the guests only have you as a choice, speed counts. Each guest you satisfy is future money in your pocket. Don't ever think you are fast enough.

  In 1977 when I started as a crew member for Rax Restaurants the fun position everyone wanted to work was the sandwich station where the roast beef sandwiches were produced. Back then only 2 beef sandwiches were available, Regular Rax served plain on a 4" bun and Big Rax with mayo, lettuce and tomato on a 5" bun. Regular was made by toasting a bun, slicing and weighing the beef, steaming it 3 to 5 seconds to increase the heat and add moisture to help release flavor, placing it on the bun and then wrapping it. I once had an order for 65 sandwiches and asked the manager to time me. 8 minutes 17 seconds later the sandwiches were finished. Speed counts. BUT at one point, after I had been

MENU

there about three months a manager told me they had been considering terminating me after the first few weeks because they didn't believe anyone could move that slowly and not be on drugs! I thought I was great?! Give yourself about a month or more to be fast. But push yourself to make every hot dog correct, delicious and faster than the last. BTW, I worked for another 12 years at Rax, so I guess I got fast enough!

Stick with hot dogs rather than sausages and basics rather than fancy and develop a simple, easy to execute menu. The original Wendy's menu was extremely simple, Old Fashioned Hamburgers with fresh toppings, French Fries, sodas and the Frosty. Chili was not on the menu for diversity but as an outlet for hamburgers that exceeded their hold time. (Actually, Wendy's used visual cues to signal when a patty became "chili meat"). That meant Wendy's cooked burgers in anticipation of selling them. You get really good at anticipation cooking when you are practicing the entire shift. In those days, the manager was also the grill man. As you may know today, Wendy's has a much broader menu than in the beginning. I suggest you follow Dave's lead and start simple then add as your license and ability allow.

Now you have an idea how to portion and price your food for profitability. Let's discuss how to price your food for ease of operations. You will notice in the above spreadsheet I list round numbers on the dollar and the half dollar. I also list the exact price to the penny for a specific cost goal. When you visit your local Wendy's, you will notice nearly all prices end in .99. For Wendy's $2.99 is 3 dollars but your brain says 2 dollars. A phycological trick, for us street food vendors we want ease of service, as we are generally alone. Price your menu in as round of numbers as you need to do the math comfortability. Include the tax rate in the listed price. That means a menu price of $7.00 for a combo is really $6.60 for you and $0.40 for the taxman. (Based on a 6% sales tax like I have in Florida, yours will differ)

To finalize pricing look at your competition. What are they selling and how is it priced. Most vendors at the very least use Facebook and post a picture of the menu. See if your pricing is in line. Going cheaper does not guarantee success, sometimes it comes off as just that CHEAP. That being said you can be successful with a discounted price compared to the competition if you market price paired with quality and taste. Remember when Pepsi first started? (I don't either, look it up) They sold their product for the same price as Coca-Cola but doubled the amount of soda in a container. They kept up the price wars until the 1970's when they started marketing blind test tastes that showed Pepsi was preferred. Today Pepsi and Coke sell for the exact same amount, excepting for coupons and discounts, of course. If you want to be cheaper than the competition you will need to stress your quality and service as superior to the more expensive vendors. Then execute your plan.

Price your menu similar to your competition but absolutely DO NOT be afraid to price higher. The point of difference must be in your Guest Experience. What is that you ask??? At this point let's only discuss QUALITY. Quality, pertaining to food, means buying the best, fresh wholesome ingredients you can profitably afford and then preparing them in a food safe manner that respects the ingredient. Finally, assembling and presenting a delicious tasting neatly assembled product to the guest. In other words: keep hot food hot, cold food cold and chips crispy.

Catering

A whole other income stream for a hot dog cart vendor is catering. Catering for us is slightly different than, say, Olive Garden. Olive Garden has catering and offers most of their core menu. Their procedure is basically packaging their products in larger containers for service on site. They will package eating and serving

MENU

utensils as well as plate and condiments. The guest orders the food, pays for it and picks it up when ready. The guest then transports, sets up and serves the meal. Nearly all restaurants offer some version of this style of catering as do many catering companies.

    For a hot dog vendor catering can be more in line with a catering only company. We sell the ability to cook and hold our food on site. Where Olive Garden's food is cooling off as soon as you leave the restaurant, our food is not even cooked until we reach the consumer. Since we are cooking on site for a private function, we have a chance to broaden our menu. **Check with your health department to be sure what your license will allow.**

    Of course, you can cook and sell your normal menu. If allowed by the health department you could offer anything your cooking ability and cart will allow. For example, spaghetti using your steam table to cook the pasta, then hold it and your griddle to toast garlic bread and heat the meat sauce. Set up a couple of bowls of salad and dressing on your usual cold holding area and buy a simple dessert. Voila you are competing with Olive Garden, serving a hotter and most likely tastier product for the guests.

    Imagine a kid's birthday party. Many of the "bouncy house" businesses have a push cart as additional rental product. What if you convince the "bouncy house" to allow you and your cart to be offered as alternative to the parents cooking and serving. Just price your service at a per kid price and offer the "bouncy house" owner a cut. Consider this an investment in future sales and make certain you have marketing material showing off your normal locations.

    How does catering work pricing wise? You need to develop a menu based on a per person price. Most guests when ordering or pricing catering may not know the exact number of attendees. Set up your menu in ranges of people served. Something like this:

Putting the Cart Before the Dog

Hot Dogs	10 delicious Deckhand Dogs with mustard, ketchup, pickle relish and diced onions all on the side	Serves 5-10	$	16.00
Chili	Pirate Dogs own beanless chili to add to your delicious Deckhands	Serves 5-10	$	2.25
Chips	5 pack bundle	Serves 5	$	4.00
Cole Slaw	2 1/2 pounds of Pirate Dogs sweet Cole Slaw serve on the side or on the dogs	Serves 5-15	$	8.00
Grandma's Cookies	5 pack bundle	Serves 5	$	4.75
Soda or Water	5 pack bundle Mix and match	Serves 5	$	5.00

This menu is for the usual style catering offered by most restaurants. That is the guests calls up, places the order and you prepare and package everything. The guest shows up, pays and heads off to serve, leaving you to count money.

The most profitable type of catering is on site catering. That is where you are the chef preparing and serving food. Your guest has ordered based on the number of people expected to attend and has paid you in advance for at minimum all the food and service. I recommend a non-fundable deposit in at least the amount of the food you must purchase with the balance due before the date of service. In this type of catering the guest has purchased all the food and it is all theirs after service. Most of the time the guest encourages their friends, family or employees to take the leftovers.

Price catering in the top example at most 33% food cost. I run this cost higher knowing I am getting a big-ticket order and all the other operating costs (propane, gasoline etc.) of the order are covered by my normal operations anyway.

Pricing an on-site catering gig is where you make the most money. Guests understand paying for food as well as your abilities as a chef and restaurateur. I base price on per person plate cost and the type of service I must provide. For example, an event where I serve table side with a menu that has a total plate cost (meat, veggie, bread, desert, drink, etc.) of $6.00 I will need to keep my food cost at 20%. In other words, I will multiply $6.00 times 5 giving me $30.00 per plate. ($6.00 divided by $30.00 is 20%) and then multiply $30.00 by the expected guest count. A party of 20 guests would cost the host $600.00. Remember, catering could include food you normally don't sell, and prep time will be increased, especially with a broad menu. I want plenty of room for profit when I price these events. Catering can be complicated as each event is completely different. Today you may only cook while the guests serve themselves, next week you have to serve the guests table side. Price accordingly. If you need help, contact me I'll walk you thru the process.

    In both my restaurant and street vending career I have done a ton of on-site catering. It requires much planning and discipline to execute a successful event. Just watch any chef competition that requires the chefs to open a restaurant from scratch and watch how often the real professionals mess things up. Catering is a big money maker but also hard work and could easily ruin your reputation if your mess up the wrong event.

    Your advertising should include a "We Cater" and a "Rent Me" line somewhere on your menu or cart as well as a weekly posting to social media re-enforcing renting/catering. Use your social media to plant the seeds of a broader menu (if allowed), giving suggestions and pictures of your culinary creations. Remember, you are only limited by your license and your ability. One of the "gurus" recommends you have "and catering" as a part of your business name. As if by some magic you are now allowed to cater, and the health department will ok it because you made it a part of your name. All you have done is make your business name very wordy. Olive Garden is not called "Olive Garden and Catering". Catering in most states is covered by your initial food license. Florida has a special license just for caterers. But guess what, every other food license including MFDV are allowed to cater on their original license. However, a hot dog vendor is still limited to hot dogs in Florida because of license limitations and adding "and catering" to your business name won't magically change that. A catering only license is for people that only make food in one location and in turn serve it in another location. A caterer offers no seating, delivery or take out for individual sized orders.

As a proud cart owner when you add "Rent Me" to your cart advertising you are letting your guests know the cart itself is available to rent for a specified amount of time. Advertising a "mobile kitchen" and renting it someone is another income stream for you. You in effect offer the cart, your guest rents it (paid in advance), you deliver it on location, offer a 5-minute tutorial on operation and then return at the specified time to pick up the cart. The renter is providing all the food, you provide the equipment and clean up.

Pricing this service is extremely location and economy based. You could rent by the hour, part of day or full day. Charging $75 per hour, $150 half day (4 hours) and $200 all day (8 hours) Just like the boat rental on your favorite lake. Have a contract that spells out delivery time and pick up time as well as the usual damage/lost or missing item clauses. Include a delivery checklist of all pots, pans and serving utensils with replacement costs listed that both you and the renter sign off on. This is great for a second or third cart.

Speaking of income streams, I encourage you to think out of the box in your business. Offer services that no other street vendor does. When I lived in the Virgin Islands, everywhere you looked was some type of street vendor hawking everything under the sun. T-shirts, jewelry, crafts, cooked foods, raw vegetables, coconuts, pretty much anything a tourist would want. In that environment selling hot dogs as a vendor was like trying to sell an Eskimo an ice machine in a hail storm. Plus, a lot of the coconut sellers had big machetes and I just didn't want to invade their domain with my little wieners. LOL

MENU

One of the restaurant managers I knew owned a small 6-person boat. He came up with an idea to charter the boat for sunset romantic dinners with a "surprise" stop at a secluded beach on one of the little sandy cays. The surprise stop would include dinner and drinks. After a few solo runs he realized manning the boat and tending the guests alone was nearly impossible and still give extraordinary service. He asked me to join his crew. We took on the persona of Skipper and Gilligan from the 1960's TV series (seriously, dude look it up) I was quite skinny back then and wore a red shirt and sailor hat while my friend didn't have the skipper's build, but he did wear the blue shirt with classic skipper hat. We had a few canned and very campy stories and jokes to entertain the guests but generally left them alone as it was a romantic cruise. I played steward, cook, server, errand boy and janitor and had a great time sailing the waters around St Thomas and St John while making good money.

Hot Dogs Around the USA

Baltimore - Fried bologna wrapped around a fried hot dog with mustard in a bun.

Carolina - Hot Dog in a bun, chili, chopped onions, Cole slaw.

Chicago - Hot Dog, poppy seed bun, pickle spear, celery salt, tomatoes, whole pickled peppers, chopped onions, neon green relish, mustard.

Classic American Hot Dog: hotdog in a bun, ketchup, yellow mustard, green relish, and chopped onions.

Coney Chili Cheese Dog: hotdog in a bun, mustard, chili sauce, chopped onions, and grated cheddar.

Denver - Hot Dog in bun, chopped red onions, green Chile sauce, sour cream, chopped jalapenos

Dodger Dog - Foot Long dog in a bun, ketchup, mustard, chopped onions, relish

Kansas City - Hot Dog, Sesame seed bun, sauerkraut, melted swiss

Memphis - Bacon wrapped hot dog in a bun, barbecue sauce, chopped scallions, shredded cheddar

Michigan - Hot Dog in a bun, tomato-based meat chili sauce, mustard

New England Dog: hotdog in a bun, fried onions, melted cheese, and mustard.

New York Hot Dog - Hot dog in a bun, spicy mustard, sauerkraut, red onion sauce

Rocky Dog: hotdog on a bun with grilled peppers, sauerkraut, and chopped onions.

Texas Dog: hotdog on a bun with chili sauce, cheese, and jalapenos.

Of course, there are many more, remember Google is your friend! You can make up your own as well!

MENU

Here are my best-selling recipes. Remember they are scaled to selling on a cart not for family dinner. (Unless your family is Walton sized. Yes, I'm old)

Pirate Chili

32 portions

- 3 pounds 80-20 ground beef
- 12 ounces beef stock
- 3 (6oz cans) tomato paste
- 12 ounces ketchup
- 1 teaspoon Worcestershire sauce
- 2 ½ tablespoons chili powder
- 1 ½ teaspoon ground black pepper
- 1 ½ teaspoon white sugar
- 1 ½ teaspoon brown sugar
- ½ cup very finely diced onions

Place 8oz of beef stock, tomato paste, ketchup and Worcestershire sauce in a bowl and whisk until smooth then add all remaining dry ingredients (except onions) and continue to whisk until evenly mixed. Place hamburger, onions and remaining beef stock in sauce pan on medium heat caramelize the hamburger and onions while breaking the meat down to pea-sized bits. Then add the tomato paste mixture and bring to a boil. Reduce heat back to medium and continue heating until hamburger meat is completely cooked, and the chili has reached a temperature of at least 165 degrees. If the chili is the desired thickness remove from heat place in service container. If not proper thickness lower heat to simmer and stir every often until reaching proper thickness.

Take note of the beef stock, remember I boil my dogs in beef stock before adding grill marks. This consistent, unique flavor is sales proven and downright delicious!

Sweet Southern Cole Slaw

Makes 32 ounces

- 3 tablespoons vinegar
- ¾ cup sugar
- ½ teaspoon dry mustard
- ½ teaspoon salt
- 2 ½ cups mayonnaise
- 2 ½ pounds cabbage finely chopped to 1/8 inch
- ½ cup finely chopped carrots

Place vinegar, sugar, mustard, and salt together in a bowl and whisk until sugar is completely dissolved. Then add mayonnaise and continue to whisk until all ingredients are evenly distributed. Now add cabbage and carrots. Mix thoroughly using gloved hands. Refrigerate overnight before serving.

When and if you chose to make your own signature toppings make sure you feature them prominently on your advertising. If you make it yourself be proud and brag about it often. This is one of the things to set you apart from your competition.

Search the internet for recipes that fit your location and regional tastes. New York style onion sauce or neon pickle relish of Chicago fame just to name a few. Also think about toppings that are unexpected like mango chutney, pineapple relish, cranberry-horseradish relish, candied jalapenos and anything else that tastes great paired with a dog.

Not to belabor the point but add only what your license and ability dictate. Scale up slowly as you get a better understanding of street vending and your capacity to properly take care of your guests.

MENU

Initial Inventory

Below is an example sheet with everything you need to get started for that first day. This recommended inventory will cover roughly $600 in sales depending on your sales mix and pricing. The list also gives you an idea of what your second day's purchases might look like if you expect the same sales amount. I always price shop as I am a cheap skate at heart, but I won't skimp on quality. Especially on food. You can taste the difference

Ingredient	portion per case	cost per case	projected use	required inventory	Total Cost	I/o for next day	Reorder	Cost
hot dogs 8/1 sz	80	$ 14.98	88	2	$ 29.96	72	1	$ 14.98
hot dogs 1/4 lbs	160	$ 114.08	24	1	$ 114.08	136	0	$ -
Nacho Cheese	48	$ 6.98	45	1	$ 6.98	3	1	$ 6.98
Cheddar Cheese	80	$ 12.98	133	2	$ 25.96	27	1	$ 12.98
buns	16	$ 2.28	112	7	$ 15.96	0	0	$ -
Mayonnaise	171	$ 6.98	112	1	$ 6.98	59	1	$ 6.98
relish bulk	256	$ 5.34	112	1	$ 5.34	144	0	$ -
mustard bulk	156	$ 4.28	112	1	$ 4.28	44	1	$ 4.28
ketchup bulk	152	$ 3.83	112	1	$ 3.83	40	1	$ 3.83
chili	90	$ 6.03	112	2	$ 12.06	68	1	$ 6.03
Jalapenos	256	$ 6.68	112	1	$ 6.68	144	0	$ -
onions	300	$ 4.98	134.5	1	$ 4.98	165.5	0	$ -
cole slaw	106	$ 4.98	128	2	$ 9.96	84	1	$ 4.98
chips	50	$ 12.72	46	1	$ 12.72	4	1	$ 12.72
Fritos	50	$ 12.72	16	1	$ 12.72	34	0	$ -
soda (Coke 12oz)	35	$ 10.98	37	2	$ 21.96	33	1	$ 10.98
water (Zephyr. 16 oz)	40	$ 4.98	73	2	$ 9.96	7	1	$ 4.98
cookies	42	$ 12.58	8	1	$ 12.58	34	0	$ -
hot dog tray	750	$ 7.96	112	1	$ 7.96	638	0	$ -
foil sleeves	1000	$ 55.96	112	1	$ 55.96	888	0	$ -
6# carryout bag	500	$ 22.94	90	1	$ 22.94	410	0	$ -
#12 bags	500	$17.94	23	1	$ 17.94	477	0	$ -
T-shirt bags	1000	$ 13.98	1	1	$ 13.98	999	0	$ -
sm hinged container	250	$ 13.57	15	1	$ 13.57	235	0	$ -
napkins (tall)	4500	$ 18.92	499	1	$ 18.92	4001	0	$ -
food gloves	2000	$ 10.78	128	1	$ 10.78	1872	0	$ -
Paper Towels	6	$30.88	0.25	1	$ 30.88	5.75	0	$ -
hand soap	2	$11.87	0.1	1	$ 11.87	1.9	0	$ -
dish soap	1	$4.98	0.1	1	$ 4.98	0.9	0	$ -
sanitizer	1	$5.28	0.1	1	$ 5.28	0.9	0	$ -
sanitizer test kit	1000	$15.90	4	1	$ 15.90	996	0	$ -
degreaser	1	$6.84	0.1	1	$ 6.84	0.9	0	$ -
film wrap	1	$4.98	0.001	1	$ 4.98	0.999	0	$ -
trash bags 33 gal	250	$29.80	3	1	$ 29.80	247	0	$ -
ice	1	$1.75	4	4	$ 7.00	0	0	$ -
			Total		$ 596.57			$ 89.72

SUPPLIERS

I was always a kid trying to make a buck. I borrowed a dollar from my dad, went to the penny candy store, bought a dollar's worth of candy, set up my booth, and sold candy for five cents apiece. Ate half my inventory, made $2.50, gave my dad back his dollar. **Guy Fieri**

Suppliers provide you as a food vendor with either inventory**, supplies or services** to run your business. Finding inventory could be as easy as going to your supermarket and buying what you need. The trick is buying at a price to maximize your profits. If you live in a small, rural area you will be limited on choices of suppliers. Get to know the grocery store managers and ask for bulk pricing. Ask for heads up on sales pricing of the items you use. Offer discounts or free meals to the manager for the info. If sausages are allowed by your state, talk to butchers for bulk pricing, they may even cut deals on hot dogs too. Local bakeries for buns, of course. If you live a larger area you have more choices such as larger grocery stores, Sam's Club or Costco and of course, Restaurant Depot. You could also set up an account with a food distributor such as Sysco, Cheney Brothers and others. My recommendation is if you go this route make absolutely certain you

SUPPLIERS

can't beat the prices elsewhere. Also, pay COD. Credit lines, while convenient, are a time bomb ticking away. Remember your business is weather driven, so ordering $1000.00 worth of supplies and then facing 3 weekends of rain and you are in panic mode to pay that 1% 10 net 30 invoice.

Here are a few of the larger food distributors in the US:

- http://www.sysco.com/
- http://www.cheneybrothers.com/
- http://www.fsafood.com/
- http://rfsdelivers.com/
- www.usfoods.com
- https://www.gfs.com

This site lists regional distributors as well. These smaller ones offer more personal service and tend to work with better with smaller accounts. https://totalfood.com/food-distributors/

I live in an area that only has a Sam's Club. I use the online ordering from my home, place the order and pick it up the next day. I am used to ordering days or even weeks ahead. As back up I have used Winn-Dixie and Publix, as well as, Walmart. Sam's runs out far too often for my liking and I have a backup in mind, always.

Comparison shop every time you shop for the family. Don't be afraid to ask for a discount. You never know! When I worked for Quiznos I discovered that I could buy the EXACT same pepperoni and diced chicken at Sam's Club much cheaper than the Quiznos required distributor charged.

On the next two pages you will see a supplier list for you to set up, as well as, an inventory report based on my menu from the previous chapter. Remember change what you want. I can set up a specific spreadsheet for you if needed, just ask.

Approved Supplier List

Primary Supplier						
Phone						
Website						
Product	Price	Product	Price	Product	Price	

Secondary Supplier						
Phone						
Website						
Product	Price	Product	Price	Product	Price	

Backup Supplier						
Phone						
Website						
Product	Price	Product	Price	Product	Price	

Backup Supplier						
Phone						
Website						
Product	Price	Product	Price	Product	Price	

SUPPLIERS

Ingredient & web link	portions/case	cost	Opening Inv	Purchases	Closing Inv	Used	Waste	Sold
hot dogs 8 to 1								
hot dogs 1/4 lbs								
nacho cheese								
shred cheddar cheese								
buns								
chili								
Jalapenos								
ketchup bulk								
mayonnaise								
mustard bulk								
relish bulk								
onions								
cole slaw								
chips								
Fritos								
soda (Coke 12oz)								
water (Zephyrhills. 16 oz)								
cookies								
hot dog tray								
foil sleeves								
6# carryout bag								
#12 bags								
T-shirt bags								
sm hinged container								
napkins (tall)								
food gloves								
degreaser			Date:					
dish soap			Staple all receipts to back					
film Wrap			Notes:					
hand soap								
paper Towels								
sanitizer								
sanitizer test kit								
trash bags 33 gal								

Putting the Cart Before the Dog

A daily inventory sheet is something you should use to help control your costs and track your food usage. I use it and it helps me control my food costs as well as waste. You are going to generate waste, from dropped food, mistakes and over prep. The trick here is to expense it as a budget item. The only restaurant chain I worked for that had an expense line for waste was Burger King. We were allowed .60% of sales as a waste expense. Why you ask? First, it is impossible to maintain SOS (speed of service) if you only cook to order. Or you could adopt the slogan "It's not old till it's sold" like some franchisees. Second, if you don't track and account for waste it hits you on food cost. Now you are thinking a cost is a cost and it reduces profits. You are correct! BUT, investigating a high food cost that includes your untracked waste means you aren't sure if over cooking or over PORTIONING is the problem. Yes, you are going to make something incorrectly and have to replace it. If you budget waste, you don't fret as much when a mistake happens because you expected and already accounted for it. Using the .60% as a guideline, sales of $1260 (there's that number again) means the waste budget is $7.56 or almost 9 FULLY DRESSED 8 to 1 hot dogs. Pretty easy to control since if I over cook I can just stay open later until I sell out as long as the quality is great.

When you purchase your supplies at Sam's for instance, you need to pack them to maintain the proper temperature all the way to your cart location. I have seen a number of inspections (you can see these online in many states) from the health department where product did not meet the proper refrigerated holding temperature. The excuse (which in Florida is, also, included on the inspection itself) given "I just bought these from the store and brought them straight here." You, as a food service professional, are responsible for the proper storage, holding and serving temperatures of all food in your possession at all times. Clearly these operators did not pay attention in Serv-safe classes and are showing their guest via the inspection report they are too dumb to refrigerate meats.

SUPPLIERS

The last thing on sourcing product is how much will you need. I base everything I order on real numbers. I don't guess when ordering. I look at what I have on hand, compare that to what I project I will do in sales and order exactly what I need.

Ordering at Wendy's in the USVI was a complete nightmare. We had to place an order with a distributor in Jacksonville FL, arrange a trucking company to bring a 20' shipping container to Jacksonville, wait for the distributor to fill it and then take it back to the ship yard in Fort Lauderdale FL, arrange passage on a container ship and then hire another trucking company to pick up the container and bring it to the restaurant once the ship docked. Now to maximize the cubic feet in the container we had to order what food we needed, as well as, figure out the cubic feet each product would occupy in the container, because a freezer container cost $1100 (in 1991) to ship whether it was full or empty. If we over ordered, whatever did not fit inside was not shipped. No matter what it was. So, if I ordered 200 cases of burger meat and there was no room on the container, guess what, Wendy's served no burgers. Now to further complicate things, the turnaround time was from order date to receive date was 9 to 11 days. The container would last about 3 weeks. That means I was ordering my next food container with less than one third of what was just received sold to my guests. I was the only Wendy's on St Thomas. If I ran out of something I had to borrow from stores in St. John or St Croix. So, get in a car, go to the docks, wait on the ferry (to St John) or plane (St Croix), walk to the store in St John or take a taxi to the store in St Croix, get what I needed and reverse everything you just read to get back. Running out was not an option. This was in 1991, well before modern home computers. I wrote a program in Basic on a Commodore 64 computer to help me order what I needed, not run out and still fill the container up. Oh yeah, I also had to do this with dry goods too. I know how to project and anticipate sales and project inventories. I can help you, too, just ask.

On the other side of the coin I have had to place orders when cash flow was a huge problem. Many days I would pray the truck would show up well after dinner just, so I would have enough cash to pay for what I needed. I have even had to refuse parts of orders because I simply did not have enough cash on hand. Once I used every paper bill the store had in the safe and cash drawers to pay for food I desperately needed. Then when a guest paid for something that required folding money as change I ran to the convenience store to break a twenty. I lived the "robbing Peter to pay Paul" life a time or two in some restaurants until I got it under control. And I always did. I do whatever it takes, and I want to teach you to do the same!

Zig Ziglar says, " *Yes, it's absolutely true that anything worth doing is worth doing poorly - until you can learn to do it well.*" You will get to be great doing this business if you take it seriously and don't allow an obstacle to end your dream. Learning profitability, how to order, great guest service and sales building techniques are really easy. The real trick day in and day out is to work like you are trained and make small improvements. Baby steps in other words.

My goal is to teach how to run a cart AND explain why things are done in a certain way. You can learn and succeed from the very first day of operations and not just tread water. Sounds like a sells pitch?!? Don't worry, I don't sell information I sell food.

Commissaries

Commissaries are, to some people, a dirty word. A commissary (or "servicing area" as in the FDA code most states have adopted) is a business that has been inspected by the same department as your food license. In Florida, we have 3 DIFFERENT departments that inspect food selling businesses. Thus, your license must match your commissary. That is why you need to line up a commissary

SUPPLIERS

BEFORE cart purchase and submitting applications for licenses. Many states require you to list your commissary on the application. (Florida does)

    A commissary is a place where you will, at the very least, clean your pots and utensils and dispose of waste water. Your state may require all your food related supplies be stored there as well as your cart. **All food prep** must be done here or on your cart. **NOTHING MAY BE PREPPED AT HOME.** In fact, the FDA code is so against this practice that it is mentioned in 3 different areas. There are "pros" out there that claim vendors can do prep at home, adding the wink-wink caveat, **don't get caught**!? This same "pro" screams about Constitutional rights (which are laws) affording vendors the opportunity to vend, but comments in live streams and in his "private" group (that has membership costs) to just ignore food safety laws if they are inconvenient. That must be why the group is private as they discuss illegal and unsafe practices. Now I wonder, what other shortcuts this "pro" takes when wearing his "I'm a cart manufacturer" hat? I am sure there are regulations that are a pain to follow in that business too. Do you follow all the OSHA regulations when manufacturing carts? Or do you just **encourage** others to not follow rules?

    I am telling you **DO NOT PREP AT HOME**. Don't do it. You are breaking the law and if a person gets sick, guess what you are now personally liable and gave your insurance company an "out" to not cover you. Illegal activity voids your insurance coverage. The very first thing a health inspector will do with a food borne illness is determine the food, the seller, how it was handled and who the original producer may be. All to make sure the outbreak is as limited as possible. I have dealt with food borne illness a few times. In each case my record keeping, operations and inspections vindicated my restaurants and shifted the investigation toward the real culprits. Usually the original food producer or mishandling (time and temperature abuse) by the distributor. Look at the recent

Putting the Cart Before the Dog

food borne illness cases at Chipotle and where the investigation led. Now, do you think not having a commissary or properly using one is a smart business decision?

The "pro" training cart seller teaches in Pennsylvania you are allowed to use a home kitchen as your home base/commissary for your cart and catering business. Well, PA calls this a "limited food establishment" and the limitation is according to http://www.agriculture.pa.gov:

> "Generally, the types of production that can occur in 'limited food establishments' (whether an actual home-use kitchen or a kitchen designed in a residential fashion) are limited to foods that are not **'time and temperature controlled for safety' (TCS) foods (i.e., potentially hazardous foods, 'PHF')**. TCS foods are foods that will support the growth of pathogenic microorganisms and require temperature controls (kept hot or cold). TCS foods can only be produced in a licensed / registered 'commercial' food establishment kitchen that meets the full regulatory code requirements, including separation from residential-use areas, and adequate plumbing fixtures."

You will need to be **inspected** in your home kitchen but guess what that bold part limits your menu. TCS includes:

- milk and dairy products
- Eggs
- meat (beef, pork, and lamb)
- poultry
- fish, shellfish and crustaceans
- baked potatoes
- tofu or other soy protein
- sprouts and sprout seeds
- sliced melons
- cut tomatoes & cut leafy greens
- untreated garlic-and-oil mixtures
- cooked rice, beans, and vegetables

SUPPLIERS

This is Pennsylvania's way of controlling Cottage Foods (you will learn about this later). Amazingly the "pro" mentions this as a way to get started no commissary needed. Except, well, super limited menu, few condiment choices and your home is open to state inspectors.

There are, however, several other states (PA included) that allow you to have a separate kitchen from your home kitchen and have that separate kitchen licensed and inspected for use as a commissary without the restrictions on food prepared. Those states have differing rules like completely separate building or the kitchen must be completely separated from the rest of the house with its own entrance or not using "home" appliances but requiring commercial grade equipment. Of course, in this situation HOA's, zoning laws and building codes have to be met.

You can set up your own commissary as long as you meet your states minimum requirements. It could be as easy as hand wash sink, 3 compartment sinks, employee bathroom and a waste water dump sink. Then you have to meet the local building and commercial zoning laws, but it can be done and surprisingly cheaply.

There was a vendor in my city that used to set up at a Grey Hound Bus terminal. He tried to fly under the radar thinking no one would notice him. He used the commissary to get licensed and never used it again. He only sold to passengers and closed as the buses left. Since we only get a couple of buses a day here he made just enough to reopen the next day. Some states may never inspect your cart after the initial inspection. Florida, however, inspects at minimum annually and he was caught filling water for his cart from the bathroom sink at the bus station. I still cringe thinking about how many people probably got mild food poisoning and blamed the bus ride rather than the food.

Putting the Cart Before the Dog

Some state requires logs be signed at the commissary by both the commissary official and the street vendor. Guess who gets blamed for a food borne illness if the logs indicate your last visit was not recent enough compared to the complaint date.

So where do you find a commissary? Try these websites:

http://www.culinaryincubator.com

https://www.yourprokitchen.com

http://www.icyprofits.com/commissaries.htm

http://www.cookithere.com/

Use Google and search "shared kitchens", "shared commercial kitchen" and obviously "commissary for food vendors".

My area does not have a local advertised commissary. The closest one is 47 miles from where I set up and 78 from where I live. Not really convenient. The closest one to my home is 42 miles away but 61 from my set up. Again, not really convenient. So, what did I do you ask? Being in the restaurant business already I know lots of restaurant managers and owners. Finding space was not hard. Start with these, just make sure they are licensed by the same agency you will be.

- Bars that open only in the evening
- Check with your health department they might help
- Churches
- Convenience Stores
- Day cares (with an inspected kitchen obviously)
- Dinner Theaters (here again only open in the evening)
- Eastern Star Lodges
- Elk Clubs
- Grocery Stores (especially if you buy from them)

SUPPLIERS

- Local small restaurants with limited operational hours
- Masonic Lodges
- Moose
- Nursing Homes
- Rotary Clubs
- Shriners
- Sam's Club
- Start your own (some states require very little to qualify)
- VFWs

You can even research existing vendor's licenses. In Florida, the search is available online. You can get a sense of who offers commissary services if you notice the same address on different vendors.

How much should you pay? As little as possible! In some cases, you can negotiate the price to nothing or next to nothing. If you find an inspected church, you could offer to do a monthly fund raiser or offer to cater after services meals. At a grocery store, offer to use them as exclusive suppliers in exchange for commissary use. Offer meals to managers and discounts to employees. Just remember anything you offer must be balanced by what you get in return. For example, one commissary charges $17.00 an hour with a minimum 8 hours monthly. That is $136 a month at least. So, if I talk to a church and can get it for free, at most, I would offer $136 in service and food, otherwise the commissary is a better deal. Another local commissary is a straight $10.00 an hour no minimum but they want to be listed on a $1,000,000 general liability policy. Since that is the requirement I add the cost of insurance into my negotiating. So, I am open Friday, Saturday and Sunday and spend about 90 minutes daily in the commissary. Times 4 weeks in most months is 18 hours or $180.00 add in the monthly cost of insurance (about $25) and you have a $205.00 limit for your negotiations. You want the lowest price (in trade or dollars) possible when you talk to someone that doesn't normally offer commissary services.

Check with your local health department on commissary requirements. I have heard of some (and that means a very few) counties that will waive the commissary requirement if you purchase food daily, discard all leftovers and have the proper number of sinks. I do not know how true this may be. My questions are 1) where do you clean your pans? Even using pan liners, the sinks on most carts are too small to properly wash anything above a 1/9 sized pan. 2) Where do you dump your waste water and trash? 3) How much can you really afford to discard on a daily basis? Because that in effect becomes your commissary cost. Another thing to bear in mind is if your inspector today waives the requirement, he may not always be your inspector, the next one may actually enforce the code and prohibit you from vending until you secure a state approved commissary.

As we are editing this book for publication in late 2017 another potential food borne illness outbreak hits the news. Again, involving a Chipotle restaurant, this time in Virginia. The issue involved several guests reporting norovirus like symptoms. Chipotle did the responsible thing and closed the restaurant for cleaning and informed the local health department. However, as a result, Chipotle's stock dropped 7% in one day.

According to mayoclinic.org norovirus symptoms include:

- Nausea
- Vomiting
- Abdominal pain or cramps
- Watery or loose diarrhea
- Malaise
- Low-grade fever
- Muscle pain

SUPPLIERS

Now pay close attention to this again from the Mayo Clinic:

> "Signs and symptoms usually begin 12 to 48 hours after first exposure to the virus and last one to three days. You may continue to shed virus in your feces for up to two weeks after recovery. Viral shedding may last several weeks to several months if you have an underlying health condition."

And the number one listed way to contract norovirus:

- Eating contaminated food

As generally disgusting as that sounds when you put the symptoms together with the causes, do you really want to buy or eat at a cart with no way to wash their hands? Do you want to purchase a cart from a self-proclaimed "industry leader" that offers a cart with no sink simply because it is not **required** in every state? An industry leader by definition, sets the standards that others follow, exceeding governmental safety standards and customer expectations.

"But they are wearing gloves and using tongs and deli paper", you say. Look at the number 3 cause from the Mayo Clinic:

> "Touching your hand to your mouth after your hand has been in contact with a contaminated surface or object."

This is how you make yourself sick. Now, just suppose for a minute the street vendor used the restroom, washed his hands and on returning to his cart proceeded to glove his hands to start cooking for the day. All good you say? How did the vendor get out of the restroom? Door knob? Wonder if the person BEFORE them washed their hands? Have you ever put on a pair of gloves without touching the exterior of the glove in some fashion with one or both hands? The tighter gloves that resemble a surgeon's gloves are near impossible to put on without touching and then adjusting the exterior for comfortable fit. Thus, the clean hands that picked up something from the dirty door knob have transferred that something to gloves and eventually your food. That is why, my friend, the FDA code requires a "double wash" after each bathroom visit. The states that chose to not enforce this part of the code are simply gambling with your business and your guest's health.

If you are unwilling to spend the extra money to be sanitary don't bother buying any cart. Low sanitation standards mean low quality food and little to no repeat guests. If one of them gets sick it means no more business. You won't lose 7% in a day you will lose it all.

LOCATION

Our greatest weakness lies in giving up. The most certain way to succeed is always to try just one more time. **Thomas A. Edison**

      This will literally make or break your hot dog cart. Location is where you will set up and sell. Obviously, a poor location equals food waste and business failure. Depending on how deep your pockets are will dictate how long you will be open for business. Commissaries are just a pain to find in some areas and too expensive in others. In both cases take a "boots on the ground" approach. DO NOT waste everyone's time (including yours) attempting to secure location or commissary over the phone. In person is always better and take a portfolio of pertinent business-related information, insurance, advertising, etc. as it demonstrates a certain level of professionalism and legitimacy.

      As in real estate location is everything. It can be the difference in massive success and tremendous failure. Be located in the right area but the wrong side of the street and you could fail. I used to run a Burger King that sat directly next to a McDonalds. The McDonalds averaged around a million a year, (I know because I also worked for them) while the BK when I took over averaged about $550,000. I was there only a few months before the company moved me to another location but the impact I had on crew moral, cleanliness and service translated into a 18% increase in sales over the previous year. I have no doubt I could have gotten it near the million-dollar mark if left there long enough. The location was good, McDonalds proved that. The past managers attitude was creating the failure. The previous managers always joked about it being a ghetto store in a dying area. Negative Nelly attitudes, even as jokes, are self-fulfilling prophecies. I never put down the store and got rid of employees that kept the bad attitudes. The Vice President of Operations (Mark Ordway, the best restaurant operator I've ever met) on a visit, pulled me aside and remarked, "Bill, there is something wrong here." Of course, I panicked thinking I was missing something. He continued, "You are fully staffed, the crew is smiling and both front and drive thru are busy and I thought we needed to close this one!" The moral of this story is simple. **Slow business does not necessarily mean your _location_ is the problem.**

So how do you find a good location? Research. I will give you a list of locations to start investigations. Amazingly this is not an all-inclusive list, give it a little thought and you will add more yourself.

I will also give you a checklist (page 84) to help you narrow the search and a video on YouTube on how to use the checklist.

LOCATION IDEAS

Daily set ups

1. Amtrak Station
2. Antique Shops
3. Auto Parts Stores (O' Riley, AutoZone, NAPA)
4. Beaches
5. Best Buy
6. Boys and Girls Clubs

LOCATION

7. Bus Station
8. Business parks
9. Call centers
10. Car Wash (esp. ones that wash while you wait)
11. City hall
12. City parks
13. Clothing stores
14. Colleges
15. Construction sites
16. Court houses
17. Daily enclosed flea markets
18. Department Stores (local ones)
19. Drug Stores (Walgreens, CVS)
20. Everything's A Dollar Stores
21. Gas Stations with no self-serve food service
22. General Merchandise store (Dollar General, Family Dollar)
23. Grocery Stores
24. High Schools
25. Home Depot
26. Hospitals
27. Hotels/Motels
28. Industrial parks
29. Large doctors' offices
30. Large Factories
31. Liquor stores
32. Local Furniture Stores
33. Lowes
34. Lumber Yards
35. Manufacturer sites (auto, etc.)
36. Medical centers
37. Medical Marijuana stores
38. Military Base (PX, Commissary)
39. Mini-golf or other small recreational areas with no food service

40. Municipal parking lots
41. New car lots (often grouped together)
42. Night schools
43. Office complexes
44. Outdoor shops
45. Outside Gate of Military Bases
46. Police stations
47. Private schools
48. Recreational Marijuana stores in those states
49. Regional Airport
50. Sam's/Costco
51. Small local Hardware (Ace)
52. Sports complex (Little League, soccer, football)
53. State parks (weekends will be strong)
54. Street vendor Food court areas (i.e. Portland Washington has Food Pods)
55. strip shopping centers with little or no food service
56. Target
57. Tourist shops
58. Truck stops
59. Used car lots
60. Vacant lot with foot traffic/ easy access for cars
61. Walmart
62. YMCA
63. Zoos with little food service

Weekly

1. Auction Houses
2. Bars (Friday and Saturday nights)
3. Dance clubs (Friday and Saturday nights)
4. Farmers market (Friday thru Sunday)
5. Highway rest areas (Weekends, Holidays)
6. Large multi neighbor yard sales (Saturdays)
7. Large RV Resorts (Friday thru Sunday)

LOCATION

8. Large Salvage Yards (Saturday)
9. Local firework events at resort areas (whatever night)
10. Marinas (Saturday and Sundays)
11. New car dealerships "tent" events (Usually weekends)
12. Off ramps {make sure safe, legal and has space} (Weekends, Holidays)
13. Outdoor movie events (usually Friday or Saturday nights)
14. Plant Nurseries (weekends)
15. Race tracks (usually Saturdays)
16. State Parks (weekends)
17. Swimming pools (Saturday and Sunday)
18. Weekend flea markets (Saturday and Sunday)

Monthly

1. Craft fairs
2. Downtown side walk events
3. First "day" events i.e. First Friday
4. National Guard Armories

Special Events

1. Air shows
2. Annual festivals (every area has something or several)
3. Antique Fairs
4. Auctions
5. Book fairs
6. Boy/Girl Scout camping events
7. Car Shows
8. Christmas Light shows both public and residential
9. Church Events
10. Club Events I.e. Rotary, Shriners, Masons etc.
11. Comic conventions
12. Cos-play events
13. County 4H fairs

14. County Fairs
15. Cultural Fairs
16. Dance Recitals
17. Estate Sales
18. Firework displays (Fourth of July, Labor Day, Memorial Day)
19. Golf tournaments
20. Gun shows
21. High school reunions
22. Home Shows
23. Local parades (Christmas, Veterans Day, etc.)
24. Motorcycle gatherings
25. Music Festivals
26. Music School Recitals
27. Nonprofit groups Fund Raising events (Trash or Treasure sales etc.)
28. Partner with kid's party rental store/cross advertise
29. Relay for Life and other charitable events (walking fund raisers etc.)

There you go 114 possible locations. More if you break up the groups listings like New car lots, Drug stores or charitable events. You will need a solid mix of regular setup locations and annual events to make the most profit. Regular setups provide the steady cash flow to pay the bills, reinvest in your business and pay you. Special events pay for the fun things like trips to Disney World. Or you could just work only the big events and still live quite nicely. I know a vendor that only works a First Friday monthly event in Texas and makes all the money he needs. He works super hard from 5pm on Friday till 6pm Sunday and brings in enough money to relax the rest of the month. If weather affects the event he sets up at a Farmers Markets until he reaches his sales goal and then takes the rest of the month off. No, he doesn't make $100,000 a year in

LOCATION

profit but he is successful because he is happy, healthy and financially carefree.

If you want to work big special events like the ones above, you will need to have a lot of practice under your belt to execute your menu and service in a high stress situation. This is not a starting point for most folks. Yes, my first day was an event, but I had over 4 years restaurant experience behind me. My recommendation is start small and work your way up to big events. If you have restaurant experience and the confidence to work these bigger venues, go for it. These sites will help you find the local events:

- https://festivalnet.com/index.html
- https://www.fairsandfestivals.net/
- Florida specific (your state may have one too) http://www.floridafairs.org/p/6

Many of these events limit the number of food vendors or the type of foods. Get all the details before committing. Keep in mind the organizers of the events tend to overstate attendance. Also make sure there is a contract spelling out all details and your rights concerning your spot. Often verbal hype vastly differs from the contract. You need some assurance of exclusivity and a location favorable to food service. Don't get discouraged if you are told no food vendors spots are available for this year. Plan ahead and ask when the next year starts accepting applications and set a reminder on your calendar.

I have an event analysis sheet (page 79) to help you determine if the event will be profitable. The sheet provides a summary of your potential profits or losses and a projected minimum inventory required to supply the event. Going to your first event or an unknown event is extremely nerve wrecking using this sheet as a guide and doing thorough research helps take away the jitters.

Putting the Cart Before the Dog

Event Estimator

Event Information							
Event:	0			Dates	1/0/1900	To	1/0/1900
City	0			State	0		

Research and Costs							
Estimated Attendance	Last Year Attendance	Number of days for event	Event application Fee	Site Rental Fee	Additional Fees (tables, electric etc.)	Damage deposit	Event permit cost
0	0	0	$ -	$ -	$ -	$ -	$ -
Additional Insurance cost	Commission Rate %	Number of Competitors	Total Number of Hours Open	Food Event?			
$ -	0%	0	0	0			

Your Goals & Costs							
Local Sales Tax Rate %	Number of Guests per hour you can serve	Average Check Goal	Variable Cost %	Operational Fixed Cost	Projected Labor Cost	My Guest % of Attendees	Projected Food & Paper Cost % goal
0.00%	0	0	0.00%	$ -	$ -	0%	0.00%

Computation Information					
Average Potential Guests per day	Average hours open per day	Number of My Guests	Fair Share of Guests	Break Even Including Labor and Sales Tax	# of guests to break even
#DIV/0!	#DIV/0!	#DIV/0!	#DIV/0!	$ -	#DIV/0!

Fair Share Projected Gross Income		My Guests Projected Gross Income		After Event Notes	
#DIV/0!		#DIV/0!			
Tax	#DIV/0!	Tax	#DIV/0!		
Net Sales	#DIV/0!	Net Sales	#DIV/0!		
fee	#DIV/0!	fee	#DIV/0!		
Event Fees	$ -	Event Fees	$ -		
Ops Fixed Cost	$ -	Ops Fixed Cost	$ -		
Variable Cost	#DIV/0!	Variable Cost	#DIV/0!		
Labor Cost	$ -	Labor Cost	$ -		
Profit/Loss	#DIV/0!	Profit/Loss	#DIV/0!		
Percent	#DIV/0!	Percent	#DIV/0!		
Owner Hours for Owner	0	Owner Hours for Owner	0		
	#DIV/0!		#DIV/0!		
Food and Paper Inventory required to cover projection	#DIV/0!	Food and Paper Inventory required to cover projection	#DIV/0!		
Is this a paid admission event?				0	Is the set up	
Is there a guarantee minimum sales threshold?				0	food court?	0
Is there a no competition clause?				0	scatter?	0
Is there a supplier nearby for emergencies?				0		
Is there a certain food or drink restriction?				0		

©Food Vendors Reality 2011-2017

You may run across one of the so-called "pros" selling a "Get any site you want" course. Don't waste your money. **You cannot get any site.** One of my restaurants the lease specifically states we will be the only food establishment on the shopping center property. Setting up at the Office Depot is not possible as the landlord cannot rent to any other food vendor without negating my lease and inviting

LOCATION

a lawsuit. At my other restaurants where we own the property outright, nothing you do will convince me to lease you a part of my parking lot. Like-wise no private business will lease to you if the company has a policy against it. Nothing you do will compel the local manager to violate "corporate" policy. You can, however, make a presentation to the corporation and change their minds with a compelling presentation and logical arguments.

When I was still a crew person at Rax in 1979 the company had a very strict policy against promoting or hiring a manager unless they were 21 years old. (I was barely 20.) Since we did not sell alcohol this was a completely arbitrary number. I wrote a compelling letter and sent it directly to the vice president of company (Ed Ourant, a legend at both Rax and Wendy's and mentioned in Dave Thomas' book "Dave's Way") bypassing all the lower level management. He came specifically to our store and met me (a crew person) after receiving the letter. We had a lengthy conversion about the policy, what I felt its shortcomings were and what benefits the company would gain by adjusting the policy. I fully expected the policy to remain intact but days later I was promoted, a full 10 months BEFORE my 21st birthday and the company paid to move me to the highest volume store it had at the time, Charleston WV. The corporate policy was changed because I presented an argument to the decision maker in a respectful, direct, logical manner.

As I said earlier chains are not afraid of street vendors or food trucks. I have attended 100's of meetings discussing underperforming units and not once did any manager ever offer an excuse for poor sales that blamed a street food vendor as competitive intrusion. My Burger King is sandwiched (pardon the pun) between 2 auto parts stores and one summer had competing hot dog carts operating one at each store, every weekend. My sales that summer were a cool PLUS 4% over the prior summer. A well ran restaurant has no reason to fear any cart or truck vendor ever.

Putting the Cart Before the Dog

Mom and pop restaurants on the other hand don't like any competition. I have attended town council meetings where local small restaurant owners voiced many, many concerns about street vendors and encouraged restrictive law creations. Each and every time I get into a verbal throw down about how superior operations will chase away a mobile vendor every single time. Only cowards and poor operators need protection from a mobile food vendor.

The things that **WILL** get you into MOST sites are:

- Meet with the decision maker (landlord, business owner, highest corporate or public official)
- List the land owner/business on your insurance policy
- Have a clean professional looking cart
- Have great heath inspections and all required licenses to show the owner
- Promise all print, radio and TV ads include the business name and location ("set up every Friday and Saturday at Bill's Hardware on Main Street")
- List location business name on all social media
- Use a contract (several generic ones on line) spelling out rent, set up times, etc.
- If you have online reviews show them off
- Explain the added benefit for the businesses customers and your guests
- Offer discounts to employees and management
- Explain benefits of on-site meal availability for the businesses employees (less tardiness from breaks, convenience)
- Propose a joint fund-raising activity for charity as a test run

LOCATION

When I negotiate for a site I set up meeting time in advance rather than just showing up and starting my pitch. I make certain I am speaking with the decision maker not a person to "pass on" information. If during the presentation you hear "I'll have to ask ..." end the presentation and ask for the information to directly contact **that** person. I can guarantee your presentation will not translate well to the next person unless you are the one presenting it. I dress like a business person button down with a tie. I have a portfolio containing pictures of my cart, my happy guests being served and eating my food, copies of all required licenses, insurance coverages, my health inspections and mock ups of social media posts and ad copy with the business I am visiting listed prominently. I leave a one-page summary of my proposal with all ad copy mock ups, my business card and set up a follow up meeting to close the deal. If I am given a "no" I ask, "What can I do that will make you **have** to say yes?" And if I can do it to seal the deal I will.

You will get "no's" and you will get them often. Don't give up. Today's "no" may be a "yes" tomorrow. It only remains a "no" if you give up. Just ask one more time.

Final word on locations some big store like Home Depot and Lowes use a service called Street Eats Limited. It is a service that set unusual, often unfair restrictions on people that are trying to make a living. For example, you must have 2 years' experience in food service, pass a background check, all employees pass a background check, be open every day the business you front is open and submit a non-refundable $100.00 application fee. They are known to be ridiculous slow approving applications. Eight weeks or more in many cases. Here is the link for the application. http://www.bestvendors.com/wp-content/uploads/2017/02/street-eats-application.pdf

They will negotiate rent in some areas, but they are simply not worth the trouble. I personally will not deal with them because it is my money on the line and they have no incentive to see me succeed because they will just find another vendor to rob if I close up shop. Their service is one sided as is the contract.

As a side note they are owned by http://www.bestvendors.com/ a company that competes with street vendors by offering unattended vending machines and pantry solutions for offices. Check out their site, they have some cool stuff and offer more than chips, soda and candy in the machines. So, if you want to pay a company to compete with you feel free.

On the next page is a Location Analysis. This sheet will help you determine if a location has profit potential. Much of the general information you can get from real estate sales people and government websites. Be as accurate as possible. Remember you already think it is a good site just by taking time to look up the information. Let the evidence prove to you the site has potential or it does not, rather than twisting the information to convince yourself it is a good site and then wondering why you have no sales later.

Check my YouTube channel for a video on using the checklist to assist you in making your daily location decision. https://youtu.be/i87OORfYaOo

LOCATION

Location Analysis

Street Address					
City			County		State: Alabama

Location Specific Permits/Licenses

Jurisdiction	Needed	Type Required	Cost	Department Contact Information
		Subtotal	$0.00	

Is a letter of permission required from the owner to satisfy permitting?		
Does the letter need to be displayed when in operation?		
Signage laws?		
List Restrictions		

Property/Business Information

Property Owner Name		Number	
Concerns:			
Business Owner Name		Number	
Concerns:			
Business Manager Name		Number	
Concerns:			

Street Eats LTD or similar required?		App Cost		Rent		Deposit	
Notes:							
Signage restrictions?							
List Restrictions							

Research Findings

Daily car count		Posted speed limit		Near corner/traffic lights	
Two way traffic		Correct direction		Median break	

		Day	Count	Avg	Count	Avg	# Guests (within 5 minutes)	
		Mon		0.0		0.0	Residential	Business
		Tue		0.0		0.0		5
Foot traffic		Wed		0.0		0.0		
		Thu		0.0		0.0	# Competition within sight of cart	
		Fri		0.0		0.0	Restaurants	Vendors
		Sat		0.0		0.0		
		Sun		0.0		0.0		

Sq. feet for set up		# parking spots			
Closest office complex			**Final Approval Checklist**		
	Visit & Invite		Property Owner		
Closest residential			Business Owner		
	Door hangers		Business Manager		
Closest shopping			City Officials		
	Flyers		County Officials		
			Marketing Plan Developed?		

©Food Vendors Reality - 2017

Putting the Cart Before the Dog

Location Analysis

My Vending Goals		Variable Selection		Results From Research & Goals	
I will serve food ____ hours a day		Impulse Buying Guests		Guests in Market Area	0
		to		Drive By Marketing	0
I expect to work ____ days a year		Potential Vehicle Guests		Total Marketing Potential	0
		to			
I expect my guests to spend $____ each		Vendor Competitive Impact		Daily Expected Guest	#DIV/0!
		to		Range	#DIV/0!
I expect to make $____ in taxable income		Restaurant Comp Impact		Daily Guests to Hit Goals	#DIV/0!
		to			
My variable cost goal is ____ %		Marketing Redemption		Annual Projected Net Sales Range	#DIV/0!
		to			#DIV/0!
My Annual Fixed Cost Dollars are $____		Business Door Location		Net $ for Income Goal	#DIV/0!
I will have ____ monthly marketing				Annual P&L Range based on Goals and Projections	#DIV/0!
					#DIV/0!
The number of guests I can handle per hour is ____				Income Goal	$0.00
				Break Even	$0.00

Decision

Expenses			Listed concerns from above:
Permit/License Cost	$0.00	Is this cost acceptable?	
Application Fee	$0.00	Is this cost acceptable?	
Total Rent	$0.00	Is this cost acceptable?	
Total First Month Cost	**$0.00**	Is this cost acceptable?	

Traffic					
Speed Limit	0	Will be a	#N/A	impact	
Traffic light/corner	0				
Two Way Traffic	0				
Set up Correct Direction	0				
Median Break	0				

Competition		
Restaurants	0	Too much competition?
Vendors	0	Too much competition?

Projected Income			
Low Projected $	#DIV/0!	#DIV/0!	Are the listed concerns acceptable?
Goal Income	$0.00		

This location is:	#DIV/0!	#DIV/0!	You have selected the first month cost as being a deal breaker. Investigate a new location.

©Food Vendors Reality - 2017

EQUIPMENT

The stock market is filled with individuals who know the price of everything, but the value of nothing. - **Phillip Fisher**

If have gotten this far you are awesome! Take a few minutes and answer each of the following honestly. These things are what you need to do or know BEFORE spending money on a cart.

- o I know how to get my EIN from the IRS
- o I know my states requirements for tax collection
- o I know my states requirements for owning a business
- o I know my local city and country requirements for business ownership/tax collection
- o I know the health departments rules for cart design (number of sinks) requirements
- o I know what food the health department says I am allowed to serve
- o I know what I cannot sell per the health department (if anything)
- o I have talked to a health inspector about my county's interpretation of code for street vendors
- o I know where my commissary will be located

- o I know where I can and cannot store my cart in off hours
- o I have a safe secure place to store my cart that meets the state requirements
- o I know where my primary location for my cart will be and how much it costs
- o I have at least two other locations as back up
- o I have a total of all license costs and have the money available
- o I have special events where I can vend (side walk art fairs, local festivals, fairs, etc.)
- o I have the full menu I am going to sell ready to source suppliers
- o I know what on my menu is held hot and how much cooking space I need
- o I know how much basic cold holding I need
- o I know where to get **all** my supplies and I have at least one back up source
- o I know my budget for my cart

If you can honestly answer all these questions "yes", you are ready to purchase your cart. Before you get excited about cart shopping take a deep breath and consider: **Work Flow!**

A bad system will beat a good person every time. **W. Edwards Deming**

On the next page is a generic cart schematic. You will need a more detailed schematic to submit with your health department application and these are readily available on manufacturers sites or you can draw one showing details like fresh and waste water storage and where the propane and water lines run. For our needs, today this schematic is for work flow only. A quick look at any manufacturer site or Craigslist and you will see this poor workflow design. Most modern carts design still mimic the early patents from 1926 carts! So, innovation in the field of hot dog carts is stagnate at best. Basically, as regulations evolved the cart manufacturers just added the required items where ever it would fit. For example, look

EQUIPMENT

at the location of the hand wash sink. If PROPERLY used (about 20 seconds) you will spend more time using it as you would be making a 2-hot dog combo (16 seconds). So why is it usually on the opposite side from where you prepare hot dogs? Wasting time and energy to be sanitary is a recipe for making someone sick and tired!

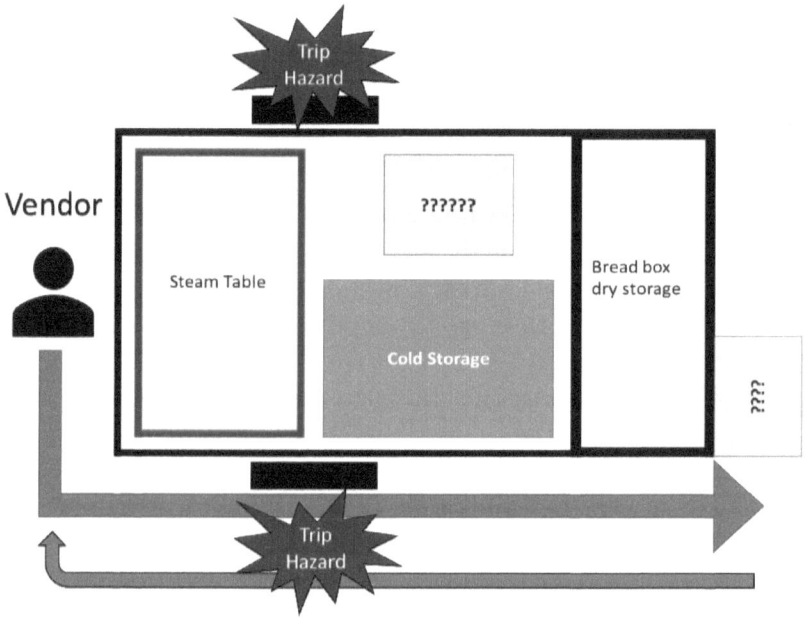

This is the popular design for the low-end carts at most manufacturers. To be blunt it sucks. The ????? areas are the usual locations of sinks. 3 to 5 steps and possibly tripping on the wheels or the fenders nicking your shins. Then the same number of steps back to prepare the dog.

How many times do you wash your hands? I am glad you asked.

According to the **2009 FDA Food Code**, hand washing is required:

- ➢ After touching human body parts, coughing, and sneezing

Putting the Cart Before the Dog

- After using the toilet; a double hand wash is required before returning to work
- After handling service animals
- After eating, drinking, or using tobacco
- After handling dirty equipment or utensils
- During food prep, as often as necessary when hands get dirty
- When changing tasks in the kitchen
- When switching from handling raw animal products to ready-to-eat products
- **Before putting on gloves**
- After engaging in other activities that contaminate hands

That emphasis is mine, if you handle money you discard the glove and must wash before putting on a new one. Reaching the $100,000 profit goal means selling at least 23,751 meals containing 2 hot dogs costing $7.00 (not including sales tax) per meal. That is potentially 104 miles you will walk just to wash your hands! All that walking is wasting time. Plus, if a guest is coming up to your cart to order they face the same trip hazard, shin nicker as you in the wheels and fenders. Cart design is important.

Besides hot holding, your cart will also have an area for cold holding. This could be where you store your uncooked dogs as well as anything else you want to keep cold. In order to achieve your $100,000 profit goal, you will need additional cold storage beyond what is on your cart. In my mind, you can never have too many coolers. You will need to maintain a temperature of less than 41 degrees for back up meats, sodas (are best at 34-36 degrees) and any other condiment that requires refrigeration like Cole slaw. Basically, three different coolers or iced holding pans at least. The trick is to set them up in an efficient manner for your food service. The first step of building your hot dog should put you the farthest from your guests, the last step should put you the closest. The middle steps

EQUIPMENT

should be in a line towards the guest. If you are moving back and forth you are wasting time and energy.

The best design is commonly referred to as "side serve" and a schematic is on the following page. Everything is the exact same size except the counter top it fully extends over the wheels and the sides extend down creating a recessed fender wheel well area like a car. The pieces of equipment are just laid out in an efficient manner and you end up with a landing space for the completed products. Put a trash can at the end of the cart for the discarded gloves and 2 steps or less puts you back to the hand wash sink. Now you don't have to walk around a corner to wash your hands. Finding a used one like this is a challenge but not impossible. I personally would a little spend more for this layout than the traditional layout simply because I know I won't get as tired working it. My wife will tell you I am a cheap skate when it comes to buying something. I want the best price but also the best value for what I am getting.

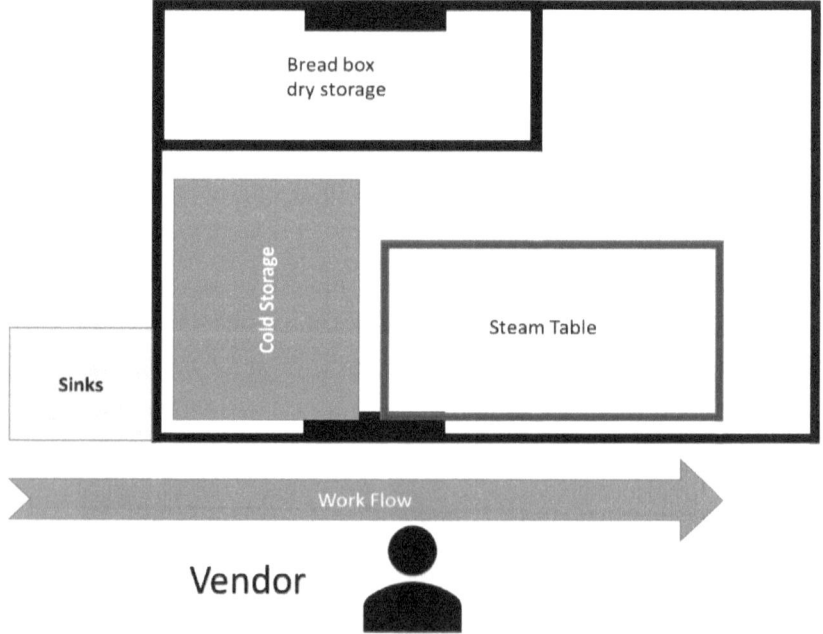

Putting the Cart Before the Dog

Below is my full setup. I can replace the dunnage rack with a 30"x72" table and place additional condiments there. I can put additional ketchup and mustard as well as a variety of hot sauces and specialty mustards. Or if need be set this up as a condiment station for guest self-service. I use dunnage racks because setting anything you are using in food service directly on the floor or ground is a big no-no. Remember your guests generally can see your entire operation when ordering.

I am rather tall at 6'3" and my wife claims I have orangutan arms. I can stand at middle of the steam tables and basically lean to reach everything. A step to handle the cash transaction, take the next order or two and start the hand-wash food prep cycle over. Easy-peasy.

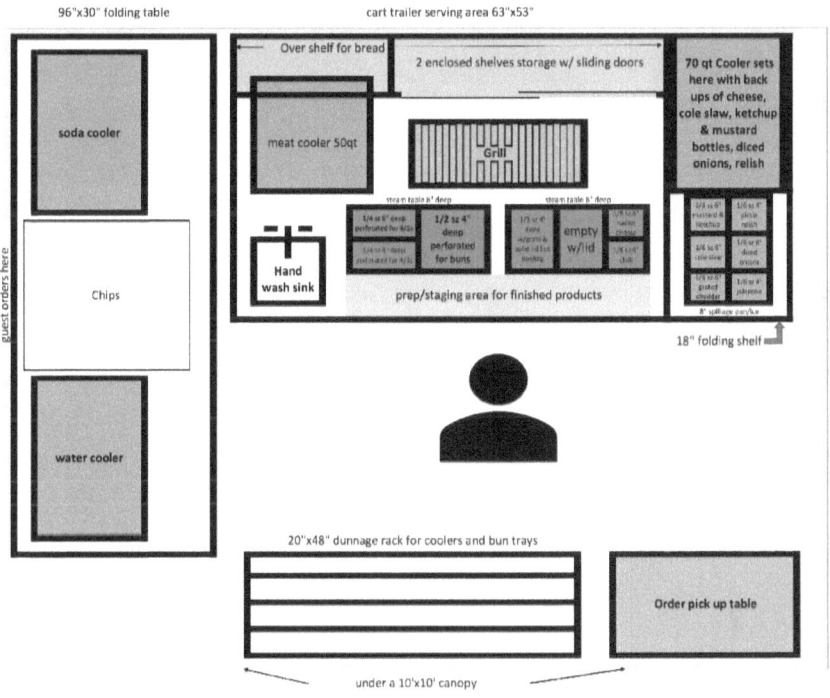

EQUIPMENT

One thing I want to touch at this point is guest ordering. Since the menu is limited, ordering consists of hot dog and different condiments. My method when a <u>line forms,</u> is to take two orders, complete the cash transaction for both and direct the guests to the pick-up area. Now I can wash my hands and glove them, complete the assembly of the orders, thank those guests and take two new orders, without soiling my gloves. Once I finish the food for these two new orders, I discard my gloves, do the cash transactions and then take **two more** orders, starting the cycle all over. I always greet that third person in line, telling them I'll be right back in a second. If you are hustling and talking to your guests, they won't mind a short wait.

This procedure is called line pacing. Since you are generally working alone the biggest factor here is moving the line in a consistent fashion. Restaurants have certain procedures that are triggered by guest flow. These procedures should help move the lines faster.

My first job was making sandwiches, but any good employee learns all the stations, that just means more hours as a crew person. This was way before TV monitors in the kitchen showing what the cashier is ringing in real time. The procedure was take THREE orders, then turn to the sandwich stations and verbally call out sandwiches with toppings along with the number of fry orders. While the kitchen is making your food, you would make the drinks, (before self-serve fountains in dining rooms) put the drinks on a tray in front of the guest, scoop fry orders, bowl up chili if ordered and retrieve the sandwiches. Then repeat. I was scared to death facing real live guests, using a cash register and remembering **three whole orders of food at once**. Never mind that as a sandwich maker I regularly kept track of up to 6 different front-line cashiers (18 total orders at once in peak volume) and the drive thru orders (we could stack 5 cars from speaker to pick up window). But boy three orders, face to face with guests, freaked me out.

Putting the Cart Before the Dog

If you work fairs or other locations that require you to have help, make certain the help knows the line pacing procedures. A good cashier can take way more orders than even a great cook can make in the same amount of time. The cashier must know how many orders to take, when to stop taking orders and what to do to help the cook. My wife is super-fast as a cashier while extremely friendly. She can bury me without too much effort. She does know when to stop and help me or face sleeping on the couch.

With the rant about work flow and guest ordering out of the way let's buy a cart. Can you afford a new one or will you purchase a used one? Will you buy one based on efficient work flow or just deal with what you can afford. Will you remove products from your menu or change cooking methods based on what you can afford? Amazingly some manufacturers consider a hand wash sink as an "extra" to be added for more money. While only a few states require a sneeze guard in addition to lids (an understandable add on item), a hand wash sink is not acceptable as an add on. Would you want to eat somewhere that has no method of hand washing? A pump jar of sanitizer is not an acceptable substitute for hand washing, and don't let these pretend "pros" tell you it is. There are three contaminates proper hand washing eliminates: physical (dirt for instance), chemical (stainless steel polish for instance) and bacterial. Guess which TWO sanitizers don't affect. At some point, someone might still get sick and it have nothing to do with bacteria. Plus, sanitizer is notorious for drying out some people's skin and causing cracks, which then need to be covered with Band-Aids. Sinks are important!

For my money, purchasing a used cart is the way to go. I find all manufacturers overpriced for what you are getting when you buy new, plus shipping costs drive me crazy. Just like a new car loses value so does a cart. Most people selling a used cart believe since it is used as a business it should be sold at a premium. Don't fall for it.

EQUIPMENT

Likewise, don't fall for new cart sales pitches. You have done your homework on what is needed to legally start your business as well as, what is required by regulatory agencies. Your cart must meet those requirements. Get started based on your budget. If you must have a new one, shop around. Factor in shipping and turnaround time. As I write this in early April 2017 one cart seller is out of carts till May 5th, claiming the next production run will be finished then. Both types of carts they sell won't be ready till then. I am thinking that is when the next shipment arrives. So that makes them a reseller, the middle man. Amazingly they are also the least expensive over all, so that tells you how much the carts are marked up. I want to buy at factory costs not after someone bumps the price. Read reviews and search for the cart manufacturer and add the word "scam" or "rip-off". Read everything you can find BEFORE ordering a cart. Every manufacturer has good and bad points, follow your gut. Checkout my blog post comparing top manufacturers.
https://moorebetterperformance.weebly.com/performance-blog/who-makes-the-best-hot-dog-cart-in-the-usa

If your budget dictates a used cart or you would rather not spend money on an asset which will lose value, by all means, start searching ebay, Craigslist, Facebook Marketplace, Letgo or any other place where 2nd hand merchandise can be purchased. Search terms include "hot dog", "hotdog", "food cart", "concession stand", "food trailer" and the usual misspellings. Don't be concerned with price as much as be concerned with lay out and condition. Prices are negotiable. I have included a checklist to help assess the value of the cart and what you should pay for it. I have videos on YouTube (https://www.youtube.com/channel/UCjQJV8DITRWvAJMngnfTZ9w) explaining the inspection, as well as, a video on searching the internet for a cart.

Putting the Cart Before the Dog

As you can see the checklist below will help you determine a fair price for your cart. One of my banker friends says, "It does not matter how many miles a vehicle has, it matters how many are left in it." A well-maintained cart should last many years, but one left in the weather, never greased, never cared for may not last the drive home after you buy it.

Ask Before Setting Viewing Appointment		Nice to Know/Have		Tools to bring	
Title or Bill of sale		Made in USA	Third wheel	Thermometer	
ever licensed your state		Removable Tongue	Side Serve	Flashlight	
name licensed under or License #		Directions:		Propane Tank	
Decision maker present				Magnet	
Gage Firmness on price				Lighter	
Original Paperwork/manuals				Soapy Water	
Includes Propane Tank?				Tire pressure gage	
Original Manufacturer/Model				Water	
Is it accessable to hook up to tow vehicle				12 volt battery	
Ask for 30 to 40 minutes to view				Towing Vehicle & Cash	

Inspection	Y	N	Est. Repair $	Inspection	Y	N	Est. Repair $
Propane System				**Road Worthy Inspection**			
propane tank			$ -	Check tail lights and wiring			$ -
with in date?			$ -	condition of tires			$ -
storage for correct number of tanks			$ -	correct air			
check lines for leaks			$ -	signs of patches leaks			$ -
check knobs - complete & tight			$ -	spare?			
Light burner & check flames				move cart by hand if possible			
mostly blue with yellow tip			$ -	wheels turn freely			$ -
				No rubbing, grinding noises			$ -
Water System				intact rust free suspension			$ -
Pump and wiring			$ -	leaf springs			$ -
correct size fresh holding tank			$ -	leaf springs good condition			$ -
correct size waste holding tank			$ -	under body rust, corrosion			$ -
Hot Water Heater (Separate)				Trailer bolt together			$ -
Check water PSI and Temp				Welds in good condition			$ -
any leaks			$ -				
correct temp			$ -	**Business Necessities**			
correct number of sinks			$ -	pans/lids/spillage check for holes			$ -
				are pans service clean			$ -
Body Inspection				Umbrella included			$ -
Major dents, buckles or metal fatigue			$ -	Umbrella in good repair			$ -
latches will hold			$ -	original "extras" bottles, ladles, tongs			$ -
plexiglass clear			$ -	Estimated Repair		$	(100.00)
interior visible rust			$				
hinges solid and rust free			$ -	**After Deal is made**			
firebox insulation			$ -	Title paperwork		secure doors, pans, etc	
cooler box insulation			$ -	properly connect/tow away			
exterior visible rust food related areas			$ -	Notes			
no attached advertizing		x	$ (100.00)				
walls contruction							
wood on wood			$ -				
metal on metal			$ -				
solid floor material			$ -				
wood floor			$ -				
metal floor			$ -				

EQUIPMENT

Negotiating a price is not a way to beat up the seller. Most cart owners that end up selling do for emotional reasons. Frustration, exhaustion, poor planning are all reasons a cart ends up for sale. Some successful vendors do retire and sell off the cart. Most sellers as I mentioned try to get premium dollar for the cart. Not really looking at what it is really worth. From a business stand point a cart is only an asset of the business and nothing more. Assets depreciate in value over time until they are worth only salvage cost whether they function properly or not. From accounting standpoint 5 to 7 years and it is off the books as an asset. It's resell value will be priced at current scrap prices. If fully functional it may fetch slightly more being sold as "working used". For comparison sake look at used equipment from restaurants. You will see it is always sold for pennies on the dollar. Just look here https://www.pciauctions.com/ and compare to new prices. For example, 1/3 size 4" deep stainless-steel pans sell for $5.57 each new or you can buy used at $0.40 for 6! Where are you getting your extra pans from now on?

Check Craigslist.org in your area, search "hot dog" or "hotdog" in the for-sale section and see how many cart ads read "I bought this 2 years ago and only used it 3 times" or "my wife wants the garage back" or the pictures show rain collected in the sinks and leaves all over the cart. Those folks bought a dust collector out of enthusiasm for a sales pitch and generally price it at near new prices because they want to recoup a failed investment and save face with the family. You can find the good, less than $1,000 cart but they are few and far between. Most likely they may need repair work and massive cleaning just to be food service ready.

Cars when purchased and driven off the lot lose on average 9% of value. After one year, another 10% is lost. By the end of year 2 it is only worth 69% of its original value. After 5 years, it is only worth 40% of its starting cost. But a cart isn't a car, you say. A cart is towed around, the propane, water and drain lines get shaken and vibrated every inch driven. Ever ridden in the back of a pickup truck? Carts don't have shock absorbers and coil springs, so they bounce around like a ping pong ball. That bouncing is transferred to all the lines. On site, you heat up and then cool down both stainless steel pans and copper lines. Water and waste valves opened and closed countless times. Stainless and copper fatigue from heat, vibration, cleaning and weather. Both will get pin holes rendering them useless. Simply put, they wear out. You, my friend, are gambling your cash on what life is **left** in the cart not what life it has led.

 Why do carts sell for so much? Supply and demand like everything else. Most second-hand carts are sold at premium prices right before warm weather. Don't shop then. Wait till after summer when the unsuccessful vendor sells out of disgust. Don't rely too much on the seller's opinion on the hot dog business. They will make it all sound so rosy and easy because their goal is to sell a cart for the highest amount possible. I have seen a good cart sell for $650 and a piece of junk for $1500 all you need to do is shop around.

 A brand new small basic cart sells for $3200 give or take plus shipping. Using the car example after 5 years the entire cart would be worth $1280. That is the full cart with all the original pans, umbrellas, gas lines, knobs and utensils that originally came with it. After 5 years, the umbrella is gone, pans are dented, gas lines leaky, water lines slimy and brittle with the original utensils missing. Yet the ad will read "I paid over $3000 and you can have for a steal at $2500." Negotiate down to the $1000 range and that might even be too high based on condition.

 I, of course, recommend buying used and as you gain ability, confidence and profits you can trade up to a new larger cart. That simply makes good business sense.

EQUIPMENT

Manufacturer Challenge

I want to challenge to all the cart manufacturers in America to produce an affordable base model cart with an **efficient work flow** design and **basic food safety** features as outlined by the FDA.

Produce a cart for under $2200.00 that has the following included:

- Hand wash sink (charging extra for more than one is acceptable)
- A Minimum 2 full size steam tables
- Efficient work flow moving from hand wash to food prep to guest delivery in fewest possible steps
- "Landing" area for finished product before delivery to guest (big enough to hold a sled at least)
- Welded road worthy trailer
- Removable tow hitch and recessed wheels (no trip hazards)
- On demand, pump driven, hot water
- Minimum 5 gallons fresh and 7.5 gallons waste water system
- Include 9' umbrella
- Include all pans, lids and inserts
- Include starter kit with 2 tongs, 2 ladles, sled, and 4 bottles
- 304 18-gauge stainless steel counter top minimum
- Sides and solid floor can be your choice of durable, non-porous materials

LICENSES

If you don't understand the details of your business, you are going to fail. **Jeff Bezos**

You are nearly ready to open for business! As the Amazon CEO says not knowing the details is a path to failure. Do you need to know everything BEFORE opening??? NO. But you do need to know enough. All of the details you have read to this point are mostly operation based. Things you will do day in and day out in running your cart. Guess what? There is still more to learn.

Food Safety

All states require some sort of food management, food handler or similar named courses. Each state also allows you a grace period to get this certification. In Florida, we have 30 days from business opening to take and pass the test. If you have never worked in a restaurant before DO NOT open until you take the courses. The test is usually packaged with a several hours class for around $150.00. If you fail the test you may have to pay to retake in some cases. Most restaurant chains use Serv-safe for both manager and

LICENSES

crew certifications. They are easily the leader in training, courses and textbooks. https://www.servsafe.com/

 Health departments generally list whose certifications they will recognize, with Serv-safe being one of many. I have taken the tests from several companies and really didn't see one as easier or harder than another. I have taken the tests in hotels, BK corporate offices and college classrooms. Now with computerized testing you know immediately if you passed.

 The reason you should take the test before your first day of business is, so you get a good working knowledge of doing things correctly from the get go. Taking the test after you have been in operations a while means anything you are doing in an unsafe food handling manner is now a habit you need to break and a procedure you must refine. Get it right from the start. No one gets sick and you have a better chance of success.

 If money is an issue and you need sales before getting the text books there are things you can do for free to educate yourself. Google Serv-safe study guides and self-tests. You will find enough information for free to begin to educate yourself. Using the questions as guides you can then Google the information and begin teaching yourself. I do recommend taking at least one class (usually 3 to 4 hours) and then taking the test. You can schedule this all same day. A good instructor will help you understand the whys of food safety. Hot dogs are inherently safe food items as they are precooked and can be eaten cold. The food safety issues arise from your health, open cuts or sores, meat based chili, dairy, hold times, condiment holding, hand washing, storage and utensil use. So, learn before you open, please!

 A relatively new requirement is having an allergen certification. Currently only a few states (and 2 cities) require formal training and certification. You can expect this to spread to other states in the coming years. Illinois recently proposed, enacted and signed its allergen training law in just over 6 months. They begin training and notification in January 2018 with enforcement beginning July 1, 2018. This is unusually fast for a change to food codes considering four states are still using FDA Codes from the last century! There are several organizations that are lobbing lawmakers to amend current food codes to include allergen certification. The laws vary wildly from state to state, as well as, the certification cost and type of approved training. Massachusetts, for example, is a ten-dollar fee and watch a video. (http://www.mass.gov/eohhs/docs/dph/environmental/foodsafety/allergen-awareness-vendors.pdf) While ServSafe Allergen is $22.00 and http://allertrain.com/ is $69.00

Beside training there are menu warnings and poster requirements you may need to meet for your cart. Whether your state currently requires certification or not, it is a good idea to at least familiarize yourself with allergen basics.

From the FDA's site: https://www.fda.gov/food/resourcesforyou/consumers/ucm079311.htm

What Are Major Food Allergens?

While more than 160 foods can cause allergic reactions in people with food allergies, the law identifies the eight most common allergenic foods. These foods account for 90 percent of food allergic reactions, and are the food sources from which many other ingredients are derived.

The eight foods identified by the law are:
- Milk
- Eggs
- Fish (e.g., bass, flounder, cod)
- Crustacean shellfish (e.g., crab, lobster, shrimp)
- Tree nuts (e.g., almonds, walnuts, pecans)

LICENSES

- Peanuts
- Wheat
- Soybeans

These eight foods, and any ingredient that contains protein derived from one or more of them, are designated as "major food allergens" by FALCPA.

Severe Food Allergies Can Be Life-Threatening

Following ingestion of a food allergen(s), a person with food allergies can experience a severe, life-threatening allergic reaction called anaphylaxis.

This can lead to:
- constricted airways in the lungs
- severe lowering of blood pressure and shock ("anaphylactic shock")
- suffocation by swelling of the throat

Each year in the U.S., it is estimated that anaphylaxis to food results in:
- 30,000 emergency room visits
- 2,000 hospitalizations
- 150 deaths

Prompt administration of epinephrine by autoinjector (e.g., Epi-pen) during early symptoms of anaphylaxis may help prevent these serious consequences.

Mild Symptoms Can Become More Severe

Initially mild symptoms that occur after ingesting a food allergen are not always a measure of mild severity. In fact, if not treated promptly, these symptoms can become more serious in a very short amount of time, and could lead to anaphylaxis.

Know the Symptoms

Symptoms of food allergies typically appear from within a few minutes to 2 hours after a person has eaten the food to which he or she is allergic.

Allergic reactions can include:

- Hives
- Flushed skin or rash
- Tingling or itchy sensation in the mouth
- Face, tongue, or lip swelling
- Vomiting and/or diarrhea
- Abdominal cramps
- Coughing or wheezing
- Dizziness and/or lightheadedness
- Swelling of the throat and vocal cords
- Difficulty breathing
- Loss of consciousness
- About Other Allergens

Persons may still be allergic to — and have serious reactions to — foods other than the eight foods identified by the law. So, always be sure to read the food label's ingredient list carefully to avoid the food allergens in question.

Permits & Licenses

More dirty words! You will need at the very least a health department license, license to collect state sales tax and a federal tax ID from the IRS. Each location could potentially require many more licenses and permits. You may need a county tax license for each county you vend within, as well as city tax revenue licenses for each city. You could need a business license for each different city and you could need a vendor permit as well. Occupational, fire inspections, tax doc stamps and many, many more ways the government attempts to tax citizens. Make absolutely certain you talk with someone well versed in YOUR area on business licenses and what is required. Again, some dude on YouTube can only address generalities and speak about their location and state. Do your own research. If you get stuck email me and we will figure it out together.

LICENSES

Insurance

Yes, you need it. You will need a general liability policy as well as your auto coverage may need to be upgraded, you may need some type of unemployment policy or a workman's comp policy. Besides protection against loss, liability insurance may be required by your commissary, your landlord or the business you front. If you have an insurance agent start there with quotes. Just remember you and your insurance agency have different financial goals. They want to sell you the highest premium policy they <u>never</u> need to pay out, where as you want the smallest premium for a policy you will <u>likely</u> need to collect. Check on bundles from your current insurance company. There are companies that specialize in vendor policies and have easy to use phone apps to change beneficiaries on the fly. Check out these guys https://www.fliprogram.com/ or http://insuremyfood.com/food-cart-insurance/ both are easy to buy and are competitivity priced.

Before insurance shopping read this article https://www.foodsafetymagazine.com/magazine-archive1/aprilmay-2013/maximizing-insurance-coverage-for-food-contamination-claims/ it gives additional information about what happens when you have to use insurance for food borne illness. Most vendors only worry about damage and personal injury because that is familiar insurance territory. Food borne illness fails under personal injury and coverage per instance can get very complicated or denied. Make sure you have all the facts before purchasing.

Record Keeping

Now it gets serious. You need to keep records for the taxman, records to measure your profitability and records to judge what venues are successful. Record keeping can be as simple as keeping every receipt, tracking mileage and giving it to your tax preparer. As long as the cash flow allows you to pay the bills, taxes and then purchase more inventory you are golden. I have a YouTube video https://youtu.be/gPUzZ8BbT1s that includes a link to a spreadsheet I have used since the 1990's to track everything I need to monitor my business, pay sales taxes and judge where I am successful and where I need improvement.

Reporting is based on what your state requires. Income may require taxes be paid quarterly and of course remitting sales taxes you collect for the state, county and city on a monthly basis. As you get your licenses for each agency you should also be given some type of "Welcome" kit or package explaining the agency's expectations on reporting and remittance. Make note of each deadline and set calendar reminders. DO NOT MISS A SINGLE PAYMENT. Tax agencies will come after you, your business and even your personal belongings if you fall to far behind in remittances. Pay exactly what is owed and pay it on time. You will sleep better, and you will give way better guest service not worrying if that police officer is there to arrest you for not paying taxes or is just a hungry guy. The second part of reporting is internal. Inventory, cash flow and location viability are things you need to track often. I recommend daily. The record keeping sheet I mentioned above helps with most of your self-reporting needs.

I also have a less detailed single page that you may find useful. Pictured on 106 this contains just enough information for many vendors. As you can see this sheet tracks your sales, purchases, inventory and waste. If your daily cash flow is enough to pay your personal bills, leaves enough to purchase inventory for tomorrow and pay sales and income taxes quarterly, congratulations you have a viable business! This reporting method is generally enough for most people and provides just enough information for your accountant.

LICENSES

Daily Cash and Inventory Report 11/10/2017

Income			Paid Out to	Amount	Paid Out to	Amount
Tax Rate %		6.00%	credit card fees	$ 4.87		
Gross sales	$	707.00	Sam's Club	$ 598.40		
tax	$	40.02	gasoline	$ 15.00		
net sales	$	666.98	propane	$ 14.88		
Total cash paid out	$	666.15	marketing	$ 18.00		
Daily Cash Flow	$	0.83	commissary	$ 15.00		
All cash paid out (attach receipts on back)			*Projected Next Day Sales*	$ 800.00	13.2%	increase

Daily Inventory Control

Item	cs cost	cs count	open	+ purch	= Total	- end inv	- waste	=sold	food cost	waste $	reorder	ord cost
hot dogs 8/1 sz	14.98	80	0	80	80	11	2	67	$ 12.55	$ 0.37	1	14.98
hot dogs 1/4 lbs	114.08	160	0	160	160	136	1	23	$ 16.40	$ 0.71	0	0
Nacho Cheese	6.98	48	0	96	96	51		45	$ 6.54	$ -	0	0
Cheddar Cheese	12.98	80	0	160	160	26	1	133	$ 21.58	$ 0.16	2	25.96
buns	2.28	16	0	112	112	0	3	109	$ 15.53	$ 0.43	8	18.24
Mayonnaise	6.98	171	0	171	171	59		112	$ 4.57	$ -	1	6.98
relish bulk	5.34	256	0	256	256	144		112	$ 2.34	$ -	0	0
mustard bulk	4.28	156	0	156	156	44	2	110	$ 3.02	$ 0.05	1	4.28
ketchup bulk	3.83	152	0	152	152	40	1	111	$ 2.80	$ 0.03	1	3.83
chili	6.03	90	0	180	180	68	2	110	$ 7.37	$ 0.13	1	6.03
Jalapenos	6.68	256	0	256	256	144		112	$ 2.92	$ -	0	0
onions	4.98	300	0	300	300	166		134	$ 2.22	$ -	0	0
Cole slaw	4.98	106	0	212	212	84	4	124	$ 5.83	$ 0.19	1	4.98
chips	12.72	50	0	50	50	4		46	$ 11.70	$ -	1	12.72
Fritos	12.72	50	0	50	50	34		16	$ 4.07	$ -	0	0
soda (Coke 12oz	10.98	35	0	70	70	33		37	$ 11.61	$ -	1	10.98
water (Zephyr, 1	4.98	40	0	80	80	7		73	$ 9.09	$ -	2	9.96
cookies	12.58	42	0	42	42	34		8	$ 2.40	$ -	0	0
hot dog tray	7.96	750	0	750	750	638	1	111	$ 1.18	$ 0.01	0	0
foil sleeves	55.96	1000	0	1000	1000	888	1	111	$ 6.21	$ 0.06	0	0
6# carryout bag	22.94	500	0	500	500	410		90	$ 4.13	$ -	0	0
#12 bags	17.94	500	0	500	500	477		23	$ 0.83	$ -	0	0
T-shirt bags	13.98	1000	0	1000	1000	999		1	$ 0.01	$ -	0	0
sm hinged conta	13.57	250	0	250	250	235		15	$ 0.81	$ -	0	0
napkins (tall)	18.92	4500	0	4500	4500	4001		499	$ 2.10	$ -	0	0
food gloves	10.78	2000	0	2000	2000	1872		128	$ 0.69	$ -	0	0
					0			0	$ -	$ -	0	0
					0			0	$ -	$ -	0	0
					0			0	$ -	$ -	0	0
					0			0	$ -	$ -	0	0
					0			0	$ -	$ -	0	0
					0			0	$ -	$ -	0	0
Remember to check variety of soda and chips. Check cleaning supplies for restocking							Totals	$ 158.49	$ 2.15	$ for next order		
							%	23.76%	0.32%	$		118.94

Contracts

Rental agreements are needed for the commissary, your site location, your cart if you chose to rent it out, as well as an agreement for a catering customer. These cover the responsibilities of each party and the costs associated. Google again is your friend. Several cart sellers offer generic agreements as do legal paperwork sites. Since they are generic in form you should consult an expert (attorney) for your state. Make sure the agreement is fair to you. As I have noted some agreements are one sided and almost impossible to follow and still be profitable.

Events should have contracts as well. When you are signing a contract for an event make certain you understand any recourse you have when other vendors break the contract, or the organizer does not live up to the bargain. Common issues not always covered by contract include:

- insufficient power to every vendor causing "brown out" like conditions
- other vendors exceed power restrictions causing outages
- vendors show up late purposely to miss health inspections
- vendors don't have basic food equipment or sanitation
- vendors clearly not Health Department licensed
- poor placement within the venue
- more vendors are present than previously listed
- falsely advertising a product such as saying, "fresh squeezed" when the product is clearly a powder
- more vendors selling exact same food type than previously guaranteed
- attendance numbers far lower than promised

LICENSES

Here is a checklist of things to complete before you open each for business. The idea is to be prepared as possible for success.

Count Down to Open for Business

Government issued licenses and permits for every location

Licenses and Permits	City	County	State	Federal
Business permit				
Tax collection				
Fire Inspection				
Occupancy Inspection				
Vendor Permit				
Ficticious Name				
Tax exempt/reseller ID				
EIN				
Health Department				
Other _____				
Other _____				

Commissary		Insurance		Location	
operational hours		Liability		signed agreement	
fees		Auto up graded if needed		rent paid	
signed agreement		Correct payees listed		second location?	

Food Related

Menu is set and printed	
Portion control understood and practiced	
starting food and supply inventory on hand	
all small wares in place (pans, ladles, tongs, knives)	
Food safety class scheduled/taken	

Marketing

Social Media	FaceBook		Twitter		YouTube		Instagram	
Print Material	Bounceback coupons				Business Cards			
Site Signage	Yard Signs				Flags		Banners	
Radio	Be part of live remote				Ads		Contests	
Guest Loyality Program								

Recording Keeping

Venue records (weather, location, guest flow)		Sales tracking method	
Inventory tracking		Waste tracking	
Purchase tracking			

Binder kept with cart

Copy of all licenses/permits listed above		Recent Health Inspection	
Insurance information		MSDS for cleaning	
Contracts	Location	Commissary	

Additional Notes

_____
_____
_____
_____

MENTOR

"My mentor said, 'Let's go do it,' not 'You go do it.' How powerful when someone says, 'Let's!'" **Jim Rohn**

Once you get open and have a few days or months of sales and events under your belt you may realize things are not running as you envisioned or the profits are not as you hoped. This is many vendors' breaking point and the cart goes up for sale. Others struggle along hoping thing get better, getting increasingly more frustrated as days go by. Unless you bring extensive food service background into your vending business, you are going to need a lot of help and advice.

You could even need help at the development stages of your vending life. The previous 6 chapters each have pitfalls that stop dreams cold. Understanding the codes, cutting through red tape, finding a commissary, getting good locations and events, managing profitability, all areas trip up good people. These are the points to seek outside help in the form of a mentor, coach, consultant, whatever the name – someone to help you.

MENTOR

We have all heard the phrase "Give a man a fish and you feed him for a day. Teach a man to fish and you feed him for life." Let's look at how a mentor, a coach and a consultant approach fishing and feeding.

A coach, be it life or business, will ask questions assuming you know the answers but are just unaware. Coaches are taught the client must set goals and figure out the details to success on their own, while the coach just cheers and asks more questions. It has been said of a coach, "Coaches know all the questions to a client's answers." A coaching relationship is a defined time period, meeting at scheduled intervals going over the client's progress. Coaches often have no experience in the specifics of a certain business type, thus they can't assist with a specific issue. Coaches may help you be a more rounded person in life and business, not necessarily operate a successful, profitable business. In the fishing scenario a coach would attempt to satisfy your hunger with questions.

- "What should you do to end your hunger?"
- "What should you eat and where would you find it?"
- "How many fish do you need to satisfy you?"
- "Where is the best fishing hole?"
- Tell you time is up and conclude in the next session

A consultant is well versed in a specific business and provides one time, usually very expensive, assistance to a specified problem. Consultants are usually retired from the industry for which they provide consulting. Consultants swoop in tell you is wrong, give you some tools and training, collect a check and leave. Consultants don't care if the tools will work for you, because they know from their own experience the tools do work. If you don't get the results, it is your own fault. Consultants, like lawyers, are generally pricey, time bound and self-serving. Arnold Glasow says, "A consultant is someone who saves his client ALMOST enough to pay his fee." In our fishing story the consultant would:

> - Give you a bamboo pole
> - Some plastic wiggler baits
> - A set of written fishing instructions
> - A map to a known fishing lake
> - A $2000.00 bill

A mentor is someone in the business, usually in a leadership role that will take someone "under their wing". Offering advice, training, time and building a relationship that benefits both. The mentor has the answers to all the client's questions and backs it up with current real-time experience. A mentor – mentee relationship is more fluid than either coaching or consulting. When the mentee has questions the mentor provides answers in real time, not a scheduled appointment. The mentor in our fish story is the one to provide:

> - the right equipment for the fishing hole
> - the time to teach baiting the hook
> - time of day to fish
> - how to clean and cook it
> - be there when you need them

The question is which works best for your needs. You may find you need all in your business at one point or another. Chose coaches and consultants wisely, both have costs and may not really be the expert you need. Mentors have little to no cost and quickly reveal themselves as useful to the mentee. If you need a mentor, try https://www.score.org/. This is set up by the SBA and can be very helpful.

You can also contact me. I want to see and help you succeed in a big way.

Operations

In the end, all business operations can be reduced to three words: people, product, and profits. Lee Iacocca

An Operations Manual includes everything you do as a food service vendor. Including proper food handling policies and training requirements, written recipes and food specifications, employee practices and policies, approved supplier lists, record keeping and cash handling and anything else the owner feels a written guide should cover. As a street food vendor do you need written policies? Short answer is "no". If you want to sell or expand, hire employees, add multiple carts, then "yes" you need one.

An Ops Manual must cover:

- People- guest and employee interactions & policies
- Product- from receiving to guest presentation
- Profit- marketing to budgeting

These three distinct sections can have as many subsections and details as needed to ensure consistency. First and foremost is the written guideline for how people should be handled. Both guest and employee policies should be written. Think of a policy as a predetermined outcome. Just like an insurance policy, when a covered incident occurs the policy goes into action with a predetermined outcome granted to the policy holder. Employee policies are exactly the same, a predetermined outcome triggered by a situation. For example, a tardiness policy explains what being tardy means, when an employee is considered tardy and what happens when that employee is tardy. A predetermined outcome. Simple. If the policy reads 3 late occurrences and then termination, it should not be a shock to anyone when termination happens.

Product handling from receiving to storage to prep to cooking to holding to serving. Each step is required by many states in the form of a HACCP plan. Operation Manuals expand on the critical points and explain the details. This makes training new employees much easier. For example, under the heading HOT DOG, the procedure would list the brand, how it is held once received (frozen or refrigerated), how it is cooked, to what temperature it is cooked, how it is held and what temperature, how long it could be held, how it is handled when ordered, how it is dressed and how it should look when presented to the guest. Written guidelines seem more concrete and are easier to train and preform.

Profits come from 2 different actions that must act in concert. Marketing and budgeting. Marketing is your invitation, asking folks to try your food. Budgeting is how you handle the money your guests throw at you. This section should include your marketing strategy, your social media policy, mystery shopper and guest survey procedures. Budgets must include written amounts or percentages for each and every dollar of sales generated. Budgets must be written before you ever sell one item and must be tracked daily. Set aside time, at least monthly (I do it weekly) to compare your budget to your actual performance.

Operations

Below is a sample product (with a recipe to try!) page from my Ops Manual.

NY Style Onion Sauce

Menu Name:	New York Style Onion Sauce
Description:	A pirate's take on New York Red Onion Sauce made with white onions, ketchup, chili powder, cinnamon, garlic, sriracha and beef stock. Cooked in commissary during morning prep
Ingredients:	4 tablespoons canola oil 4 medium onions, sliced thin 1/2 cup ketchup 1/8 teaspoon ground cinnamon 1/4 teaspoon chili powder 1/4 teaspoon garlic powder 1/2 teaspoon sriracha 1 cup beef stock
Instructions:	In a skillet, heat oil over medium heat Add onion slices Sauté about 7-10 minutes until golden & limp Mix in the ketchup Add the cinnamon, chili powder, garlic powder & sriracha Pour in beef stock Stir Bring to a boil then reduce heat and simmer uncovered 10 minutes

Cash Handling

As a street vendor, your business may be completely cash only. In order to make change you will need a "bank" amount. $75 is the absolute minimum to make change. Keep your prices as round as possible. Either use whole dollar amounts or use multiples of quarters for menu prices. On the $75 starting bank have $20 in quarters and ones and $35 in fives. This amount is prone to not having enough change if the first 3 guests spend $7 and pay with $20's. The next twenty you will not be able to break without using up all your remaining bills.

I use a starting bank of $100, the same $20 in quarters, with $30 in ones and $50 in fives. Still possible to run out early but far less likely. For big events, I keep extra change locked away in my van. I have put a sign on my cart when running low on change asking for ones or fives. Almost always my guests come through for me.

I use a cash drawer that is bolted to the underside of my guest facing table. Push the button, it opens, and change is made. It keeps my cash out of the view of guests much more so than using the apron method many vendors use. Remember I run my cart as a mini restaurant. I also use a free POS (point of sale) program called LoyversePOS (https://loyverse.com/). This is a cash register program that is powerful enough to track sales, product mix and recipes. Programmed on my Samsung phone along with my Square device it gives a sense of financial security to my guests. Plus, the receipt function of Square (they also have a free POS when you use their credit card system https://squareup.com/) allows me to track email addresses. This is especially handy for catering events. During high sales festival events, it makes tracking dollars and inventory a breeze. As well as, creating records for planning the next event.

Operations

You many also want to include a "tip" jar. One of the "pros" brags about "free money" and says everyone needs a tip jar. Well, tips are nice but are not "free" because they are income and have to be reported as such and then taxes paid. Tipping is very dependent upon social factors and area. For example, when my wife works alone she gets double the tips I get yet we both are equally fast and friendly. According to Wikipedia,

> *studies of the real-world practice show that tipping is often discriminatory or arbitrary: workers receive different levels of gratuity based on factors such as age, sex, race, hair color and even breast size, and the size of the gratuity is found to be only very weakly related to the quality of service"*

Tips are generally dropped in the jar based on change. Usually all coins hit the jar, if anything more is given it is usually a single dollar. That being said I rarely put out a tip jar. I feel as business owner the best tip I could get is a repeat customer. Besides how often have you tipped the manager or owner of a brick and mortar business? They, after all, are the ones that trained the employees and provide the environment for the great food and service. The only time I use a tip jar is at big events when I hire helpers and I let **them have all** the tips as incentive.

Record Keeping

You will need some form of record keeping. In simple terms, you can just count the cash you have at the end of your day and record that as gross sales. Then divide that number by 1.xx (xx being your locations tax rate) and the result is your net sales. Subtract the gross from the net and that is what you pay the different state and county revenue offices. Gross sales of $1260.00 divided by 1.06(Florida sales tax is 6% or .06) equals $1188.68 in net sales. Leaving $71.32 for the tax man.

Putting the Cart Before the Dog

How do you figure sales tax? The formula is very simple:

TOTAL $ divided by 1.06 (again replace the "06" with your rate) = YOUR $

Then

TOTAL $ minus YOUR $ = TAXMAN $

A common mistake is simply taking TOTAL $ times TAX RATE and sending the result to the TAXMAN. This is incorrect and will cost you money. Here is an example of how much you could lose.

	Gross Sales	Tax rate	Net Sales	Tax $
Correct	$9,061.00	6%	$8,548.11	$512.89
Incorrect	$9,061.00	6%	$8,517.34	$543.66
			over payment	$30.77

I don't know about you, but I'd chase $30 cross Interstate 4 in Orlando during rush hour traffic. If you use the spreadsheets I give you this is one mistake you will not make.

Now the record keeping gets complicated. Of the $1188.68 you have, some of it will be spent to replace your food/paper/supplies inventory, some to purchase propane and gasoline, some to pay bills (cell phone, commissary, rent, etc.). Get receipts for every expense. I staple them to the daily inventory sheet. I make it easy on my tax preparer.

I take credit cards using Square. Generally getting the money in 2 days. My sales increased dramatically when I added this feature. My tourist guests use a lot of plastic and are happy I accept it. When I first started taking cards (2011), the Square device got a lot of negative remarks and questioning looks. Now it is so prevalent no one gives it a second thought.

Operations

I cannot stress proper record keeping enough. Record everything. Save invoices, statements and receipts. It is better to over document than under. Legal pads might be a funny way to claim you are documenting expenses while bragging about how easy this business can be, but they are easily questioned. A tax preparer will accept any scrap of paper as a record and file your taxes accordingly. Now imagine you are audited by the IRS, do you really want to enter the office with a shoe box of note pads and scrap papers.

Now couple that audit with a video of you saying "hot dog vendors run a cash business and sometimes spend that cash without recording it as income. It happens all the time in cash businesses." Yep, the vending "pro" has on several live streams implied cash impropriety and even encouraged vendors to have sloppy cash accounting "because it happens all the time". I say, "INTEGRITY?".

Did you know the IRS has a manual on verifying reported sales by street vendors? This 150-page manual gives several accounting methods to verify under-reported sales and well as several cross checks designed, again, to verify sales. Amazing the "guru" does not know this or if he does is not willing to admit it and share this with his minions. Al Capone was imprisoned for tax evasion (under reporting income) NOT for all the other crimes attributed to him. Remember you will sleep better following health codes and paying your legally owed sales and income taxes.

Now, I do take advantage of every legal deduction possible. I recommend you see a tax professional for more advice. There are a ton of deductions available to business owners and you should take advantage of them.

Guest Experience

Ops Manuals always address QSC which is common restaurant jargon for Quality, Service & Cleanliness. Only one chain I know adds an "A". Which stands for Atmosphere or Ambiance. You can justify higher prices if you excel in these 4 things. Each of these are weaved into your Ops Manual with each entry no matter what category it falls under.

Let's look at the best example of great Guest Experience - Chick-fil-a. Regardless of your view on corporate policy and religion, Chick-fil-a cannot be denied as an amazing success. In per restaurant sales for 2016 they were the **ONLY** chain to top both the 3 and 4 million marks in sales per unit. (Remember, they do in 312 days a year as they are closed every Sunday) They even sell 3 times more chicken than KFC and have 2000 less locations! McDonalds average sales was 2.550 million for a distant 5th place. Above Mickey Ds are Jason's Deli at 2.609 million, Panera at 2.7 million and Whataburger at 2.706 million. Go into a properly ran Chick-fil-a and you will see the clues for success. Properly maintained grounds and building, clean dining room, properly uniformed and smiling employees that greet you **ASAP**. The employees are trained to look you in the eye and respond to a guest's "Thank you" with an enthusiastic "My pleasure!" Employees are well trained, perform as trained and the company reaps the benefits of that training in sales. Their product is the humble chicken BUT prepared in a way like no other restaurant. You can see, taste and feel the difference!

Quality starts with the ingredients, consistent cooking methods and proper assembly of the finished product so that it looks and tastes awesome.

Service is not only fast but friendly and courteous, remembering names is a way to set yourself apart.

Operations

Cleanliness is simple. Everything you touch, handle and assemble must be in a clean environment and delivered in a sanitary way. Your cart should look and feel organized. Your and your uniform or clothing should be clean. Keeping a spare shirt or apron around is a good idea. Spills happen!

Atmosphere is the overall "feel" of the operation. It differs from service in that you can be both fast and courteous while being totally robotic. Mystery shoppers often are asked to time SOS (speed of service) and then later in the report asked were they "Thanked" by the cashier. Rarely if ever is the question posed "Were you SINCERELY thanked?" Big difference. The restaurant gains points for going thru the motions by the book but the guest ultimately feels "off" about the visit. Thus, less likely to return. Atmosphere is that little "extra" that makes a restaurant extraordinary.

QSAC – Quality

As you would expect quality includes all your food handling procedures, from receiving to serving. You must source, buy, receive, prep, cook, hold and serve with the guest in mind. Ask yourself the following questions:

- ➢ Will my guests love this product I am buying?
- ➢ Can I make a reasonable profit selling this product?
- ➢ How can I maintain high quality at every step of handling this product?
- ➢ What happens when the product is no longer of high quality?
- ➢ How do I know when the product is no longer high quality?
- ➢ Will this product drive new sales or just cannibalize current sales?
- ➢ Can my staff and I maintain superior quality while meeting SOS goals?

- ➤ Will my guests purchase this product at my retail price?
- ➤ What sets my product apart from my competitors?
- ➤ Will this product be affected by seasonality?
- ➤ Will this be a limited time offer or a core menu item?

Many restaurants use some form of checklist to ensure equipment is functional and food is at quality. Amazingly other restaurants don't. Burger King requires a daily checklist be completed before each major meal period while some chains I worked for did nothing to verify holding times, cooking timers or equipment temps. Having a guest return something because it is not cooked properly, not hot or cold enough is embarrassing and usually preventable. Most of these types of complaints happen when shortcuts become prevalent in operations or staff assume equipment is working correctly. I am including a checklist for food and general safety that I perform every time I open. Besides ensuring all my equipment is working correctly, hot and cold foods are correctly held and cooked, it also provides documentation of my food standards if a food borne illness is alleged. This checklist is based on **HACCP** system, identifies specific hazards and measures for their control to ensure the safety of food. **HACCP** is a tool to assess hazards and establish control systems that focus on prevention rather than relying mainly on end-product testing. Something more to learn in food safety classes!

Operations

Daily Operations and Safety Checklist

Date				By				
Directions: Determine areas on the cart requiring corrective action. Record corrective action taken and retain on file.								
			Trailer Safety					
op	cl	Inspect	Looking for:	Maintenance Log				
		Hitch	good condition with secure attachment	Date Wheel Bearings greased:_____				
		Safety Chains	good condition with secure attachment	Fire extinguisher date:_____				
		Tires	no signs of cracks or tears, good tread	air pressure left:		air pressure right:		
		Doors/latches	locked, bars in place to prevent sliding	Lights	turn indicator		brake	backup
		Small wares	stored in van ready to transport					
			Utilities					
		Fresh Water Tank	full at open	Date last sanitizing solution flush_____				
		Waste Tank	valve "off" before any travel & on location	Empty Waste tank at commissary/sanitize daily				
		Propane Tanks	enough propane for business projection	securely attached		**TURN OFF FOR TRAVEL**		
			HACCP					

Personal Hygiene	Yes	No	Corrective Action Taken
Good personal hygiene observed			
Employees wear clean clothes/aprons with hair net/hat			
Hair is restrained (hair net/hat)			
Employees appear in good health			
Employees wash their hands between task/operations			
Employees wash hands only in approved hand wash sinks			
Employees hand wash if hand contact with hair, skin, clothes			
Employee personal stored away from cart			

Food Source	Yes	No	Corrective Action Taken
Food purchased from approved sources (not home made)			
Food prepped in commissary (not at home)			
All prepackaged foods properly labeled			
Food is received at proper temperatures when delivered			
Food appears in good condition, no signs of tampering			

Cold Holding/Dry Storage	Yes	No	Corrective Action Taken
Cold food is held at 40°F or below			
Food items stored inside coolers are covered			
Ready-to-eat items are stored above raw foods			
Food items are stored 6 inches off the floor/ground			
Opened foods stored in a closed/labeled food grade container			
Open foods are protected from contamination			
Chemical and non-food items are stored away from foods			

Food Preparation	Yes	No	Corrective Action Taken
Approved safe thawing methods are used			
Prep is preformed keeping food in danger zone < 2 hours			
Food thawing is performed in an approved sink			
Thawed foods are not re-frozen.			
Food Prep is only done in commissary not on cart			
Produce is washed in an approved sink at commissary			

Putting the Cart Before the Dog

Daily Operations and Safety Checklist

Date		By			
Food Preparation *(continued from previous)*			Yes	No	Corrective Action Taken
Food items are not left unattended					
Utensils are used to handle food.					
Cooking			Yes	No	Corrective Action Taken
Cooked food reach proper internal for at least 15 seconds					
Fruits and Vegetables cooked to 135 °F					
Whole pieces of beef, veal, lamb, pork, fish cooked to 145 °F					
Ground beef is cooked to 155 °F					
Poultry is cooked to 165°F.					
Stuffed foods/stuffing containing animal product cooked to 165°F					
A calibrated probe thermometer (±2°F) is available					
Day Dot System stocked and followed					
Cooling			Yes	No	Corrective Action Taken
Food is rapidly cooled from 135°F to 70°F within 2 hours					
Food continues cooling from 70°F to 41°F within 4 hours					
Hot Holding & Reheating			Yes	No	Corrective Action Taken
Hot food is held at 140°F or Above.					
Rapidly cooled leftover foods are reheated to 165° F for 15 seconds					
Reheating of food items is performed within 2 hours.					
Proper equipment used to reheat foods (NOT STEAM TABLES)					
Cleaning & Sanitizing			Yes	No	Corrective Action Taken
All utensils are washed, rinsed, and sanitized after use					
Food surfaces/equipment sanitized every 4 hours or as needed					
Approved sanitizer solution is available					
3-compatment sink is available when washing wares					
Sanitizer solution test kit is available					
Sanitizer solution for storage of wiping towels & tested					
Towels stored in sanitizer solution between uses & away from food					
Sanitizer solution in spray bottle set up and tested					
Cart Sanitation and Maintenance			Yes	No	Corrective Action Taken
Food preparation areas on cart are maintained & clean					
Coolers are clean and in good repair.					
Food equipment (steam table, grill) clean and good repair					
Sides, interior cabinets clean and good repair					
Hand washing facilities are accessible and fully stocked					
Food contact equipment is smooth and easily cleanable					
Plumbing fixtures are in good repair (e.g. not leaking clogged)					
Premises around cart and trash area are clean & debris free					
Trash container lids are closed					

Operations

Daily Operations and Safety Checklist

Date					By			

Temperature Log

Delivery/Pickup Temperatures				Take two frozen and two refrigerated per delivery/pickup				
Vendor		Frozen	Refrigerated	Vendor			Frozen	Refrigerated

Commissary

Freezer -5° to 0°		Cooler 34° to 40°		Hot Water 110°-120°		Fryer 350°	
Grill 375°		Oven 375°					
				3 comp sink set up	sanitizer 50-100 ppm		

Cooked/Prepped at Commissary

Product	Procedure	Temp	Secondary Procedure	Temp	Transport Procedure	Temp
Chili	recipe cooking		small batches/cool overnight		cold in cooler	
Relish	recipe prepping		wrap		cold in cooler	
Brownies	recipe baking		cool over night/cut&wrap		room temperature	
Lemonade	recipe		cool over night		In tall cooler	

On Location Cooking/Hot Holding

Product	Cooking Procedure /Cookout Temp	Cooking Procedure	Record temperature every 4 hours			
Chili	reheated min 165° for 15 seconds	hold min 140°/15 minute stir				
Grilled Onions	cooked to 135° for 15 seconds	hold min 140°/15 minute stir				
Nacho Cheese	reheated min 165° for 15 seconds	hold min 140°/15 minute stir				
8 to 1 HD	cookout temp 155° for 15 seconds	hold min 140°/30 hold time				
4 to 1 HD	cookout temp 155° for 15 seconds	hold min 140°/30 hold time				
Brat/Sausage	cookout temp 155° for 15 seconds	hold min 140°/30 hold time				
Brat/Sausage	cookout temp 155° for 15 seconds	hold min 140°/30 hold time				
Burger	cookout temp 155° for 15 seconds	hold min 140°/15 hold time				

On Location Cold Holding

Product	Temp	Record temperature every 4 hours			Product	Temp	Record temperature every 4 hours			
Onions	36°-40°					36°-40°				
Cheddar Chez	36°-40°					36°-40°				
Mozzarella Chz	36°-40°					36°-40°				
Cole Slaw	36°-40°					36°-40°				
	36°-40°					36°-40°				
Beverage Test	34°-36°					36°-40°				

Cooler Temp Log

Specs	Cooler #	Visible Therm.	Record temperature every 4 hours			Cooler #	Visible Therm.	Record temperature every 4 hours			
36°-40°	#1					#5					
36°-40°	#2					#6					
36°-40°	#3					#7					
36°-40°	#4					#8					

QSAC - Service

Service has 2 components - Courtesy and Speed. Mastering both is a challenge, if it wasn't everybody would be doing them. For example, I post a script of how I want the drive thru answered by the register they are ringing the order on. Now you are thinking that is why they sound so bored and robotic when answering the drive thru. And you would be wrong. Boredom stems from not understanding how important that position is to the company. The manager has done a poor job of creating an environment where the employees feel important and empowered to satisfy the guest. I have answered a drive thru thousands of times and if I work it longer than a couple of minutes I get complimented on my "radio voice". I don't even realize I do it now. I automatically sound enthusiastic and focused when taking an order. Like I am seeing an old friend for the first time in years. My hot dog cart service is the same. I recognize each guest by name if possible or as if I know them, I ask how they are and what they would like to eat. Something along the lines of: "Hey Joe! How you been? I hope you are hungry! The chili is amazing!" If I can tell they are tourists I ask about vacation, or liking the beach. I comment on t-shirt slogans, hats, cool cars whatever I notice and then offer to take the order by bragging about the food, how cold the soda is or whatever else comes to mind. The whole time looking them in the eye, giving full attention to what they want. As I make the order, I continue the conversation until I present the food. A sincere "Thank You, ya'll come back and see me!" Usually gets a laugh as I sound really country when I say it.

One very smart owner I knew at Burger King developed his own methodology concerning the age-old business axiom "The customer is always right". His philosophy was called "YES Policy". Basically, when asked a question by a customer the answer is always "Yes". How many times do you ask for an extra sauce from McDonalds and the answer is "I have to charge 25 cents for it." Or some other line of disgust from the crew. Charging extra for say, 1 honey mustard packet, indicates the manger has a food cost problem and they are blaming it on those pesky guests that always want something for nothing. Charging for extra is the poor owner or manager's way of saying "got'cha" to guests. They will still have a food cost problem AND now, upset guests. For every guest that wants 10 extra honey mustard packets for a 4-piece nugget there are 20 guests that want only one or none. It works out if you cost extra in from the beginning. That is why I cost my dogs as if EVERYONE wants EVERYTHING. Guess what, it simply does not happen! So, the guy that wants the extra-extra-extra-extra mustard and 20 jalapeno rings that don't fit on the bun besides everything else I offer as a topping, doesn't bother me. I know his excesses have already been paid. Remember your business goal is to extract as much money as possible from each guest in a manner that makes them want to repeat the process tomorrow. Charging for extra condiments or saying "No, but" won't create repeat sales. Service should be **FAST, FRIENDLY** and **POSITIVITLY MEMORABLE.**

SOS (speed of service) must be measurable in some manner. All the major fast food chains have devices that record information related to how quickly a guest is served. Each part of the guest experience from entering the line to order to food delivery is measured and analyzed. I will tell you some chains absolutely cheat the measurement systems. For example, one franchisor (with a clown mascot and one apparently also in the corporate office) puts the system in complete control of employees. Each part of the guest transaction was measured from how long it took to answer the window speaker to how long the order took the kitchen to prepare. As well as how long it took to bag and how long it took to deliver to the guest. Stay with me on this it may be hard to follow if you have never worked in a restaurant. Once the guest tripped the presence alert system the timer started for the cashier on the order taking register as the cashier rang in food it would appear on the kitchen screen. The kitchen could not clear the order off their screen until the cashier had completed the order and forwarded the order to the cash collection register. Once forwarded the kitchen could clear off the order thus stopping their part of the timer. At that point whether the food was prepared or not the person assigned to bag food and take to the window could then clear their screen stopping their part of the timer. Now the drive thru person that presents the food at the second window can clear their screen stopping the timer completely for that car. At that point, the car may not have even gotten to the first window let alone be given food. That is why they often mess up orders leaving products off. If a large order is taken the cashier may actually forward the order to the cash collection register before the guest has finished ordering. The cashier can recall the order to add the remaining part of the order, BUT the timer has stopped for the cashier. The same applies for each station, clearing the order off stops the clock, recalling the order DOES NOT restart it. The final straw for me was when a corporate report was proudly displayed with each of the different measurements, listing the top stores in each. The kitchen time on average for the area, was an amazing 9 seconds for dozens of stores with several stores at less than 7 seconds. All the managers and district managers were celebrating the awesomeness of the franchisee results. I asked a simple question not one person understood. "What is the speed rating for the bun toaster?"

    Dumb question? Let me further explain. In the kitchen, procedure states "buns are to be toasted when ordered." Once ordered the bun is dropped into a toaster rated for 11 to 13 seconds to toast. After the bun pops out the sandwich is prepared, boxed or wrapped and sent towards the holding area. THEN the timer is to be turned off. Giving an accurate measurement of how long it takes to produce the sandwich. Timers provide information to assist managers in providing training and feedback to staff. Cheating the numbers does not help the staff get better or help guests receive the

Operations

food in a timely manner. During lunch 9 seconds is possible just not likely. Lunch orders are small, easy and generally one meal per car. There are exceptions, such as the one person buying for the whole office, ordering several different sandwiches, all specials which of course takes time to say as well as ring up.

Staff wearing headsets in the kitchen and focused on the guest could hit the 9 second mark without cheating only during lunch. Most high volume fast food restaurants will run a kitchen staff dedicated to the drive thru as well as one just for the front. After lunch, the staffing is reduced, and the kitchen will be making both front and drive thru at the same time. Averaging 9 seconds for a full day across many stores is impossible.

Any system can be cheated. Metal detectors and radar are cheated with sheet pans adding phantom cars to lower the average, or store level management having access to remove cars from the total time as they see fit. The timer is designed to be a training tool. If the numbers are fudged, then staff training, and guest satisfaction suffer.

The biggest challenges facing the fast food industry (including street level food vendors) as a whole is Quality and Service. Until companies take a realistic view of internal metrics like SOS, proper holding times and guest comments, they will wallow in stagnate sales only to be propped up by the next "amazing, delicious" product R&D throws out. Followed by the "back to basics" campaign that inevitably follows.

I want you understand SOS and develop your own procedures to insure great service. Earlier I said if you can take and then produce a $7.00 order every minute for your entire 3-hour service it will produce daily sales of $1260. Break down the one-minute service in this manner assuming a 2-dog combo, self-service soda and chips:

Guest steps up to order and the timer starts.

- ➢ 0 to 8 seconds your greeting and offer to take order.
- ➢ 8 to 30 seconds guest tell you the order
- ➢ 30 to 35 seconds cash transaction
- ➢ 35 to 51 seconds prepare food (remember 8 seconds a dog?)
- ➢ 51 to 60 seconds present food and thank guest.

Set up your own standards for SOS based on your menu and ability. Have someone time you during your practice sessions or your first days. Use that time as the bar and improve.

Did you notice what is missing from the flow of guest service? Hand washing. As mentioned before any application of a glove requires hand washing. Here is the flow with hand washing included:

Guest steps up to order and the timer starts.

- ➢ 0 - 8 seconds greeting & offer to take order.   (8 seconds)
- ➢ 8 - 30 seconds guest tells you the order   (22 seconds)
- ➢ 30 - 35 seconds cash transaction   (5 seconds)
- ➢ 35 - 65 seconds hand washing and drying   (30 seconds)
- ➢ 65 - 81 seconds prepare food   (16 seconds)
- ➢ 81 - 90 seconds present food and thank guest   (9 seconds)

The cost of gloves for 3 hours = 240 x .0054 = $1.296 x 141 days a year= $182.74.

You are only taking one order every 90 seconds and the impact on daily sales is a 33% reduction in total number of orders per hour dropping sales to $840.42 daily or $118,499.22 annually. No more 100,000 plus profit. Sad face!

Now compare that with line pacing from the "*EQUIPMENT*" chapter:

Operations

- 0 - 8 seconds greeting & taking 1st guest order (8 seconds)
- 8 - 30 seconds guest tells you the order   (22 seconds)
- 30 - 35 seconds cash transaction   (5 seconds)
- 35 - 43 seconds greet & take 2nd guest order (8 seconds)
- 43 - 65 seconds 2nd guest tells you order   (22 seconds)
- 65 - 70 seconds 2nd guest cash transaction   (5 seconds)
- 70 - 100 seconds hand wash   (30 seconds)
- 100 - 132 seconds preparing all food (32 seconds {16x2})
- 132 - 150 seconds present and thank (18 seconds {9x2})
- 150 - 180 greet & take 3rd guest order (30 seconds {8+22})
- 180 - 210 greet & take 4th guest order (30 seconds {8+22})
- 210 to 242 seconds prepare food   (32 seconds {16x2})
- 242 to 247 discard gloves $ transact cash 3rd guest (5 sec.)
- 247 to 256 present food & thank 3rd guest   (9 seconds)
- 256 to 261 seconds cash transaction 4th guest (5 seconds)
- 261 to 270 present food & thank 4th guest   (9 seconds)

Cost of gloves for 3 hours = 80 x .0054 = $0.43 x 141 days a year = $60.91

The annual sales possible becomes $157920, an **increase** of $39421 in gross sales and a **reduction** of $121.83 in costs all by pacing your line. Shave off 7 seconds per guest in faster service and you will make up the difference towards that $100,000 profit target!

QSAC – Cleanliness

Cleanliness goes beyond the cart. Pots and utensils should look clean, and maintained. Food should be stirred often and crust free. The area surrounding your cart should be organized, clean and clutter free. If you set up on a public area you may have to police trash that is not yours, pull weeds or any number of things that have nothing to do with your cart business. BUT if you can see it, so can the guest. That McDonalds cup crushed in the gutter may not be yours, but guests see that as you set up in a trash heap and are not worried about cleanliness, therefore, your food must not be up to standard. Your uniform must be clean and stain free. You don't have to have a formal "uniform" with logos but something consistent such as a polo shirt. If you wear personal clothes be aware of your t-shirt slogan and logos. You might love your tattered t-shirt that reads "f* * * off", your guests won't. Especially, if kids are around. I have thrown out people of my restaurants that loudly curse or cause some disruption to my other guests. I also won't allow a guest to curse my staff. A complaint can be stated without being abusive and likewise handled without negative attitudes.

Your supply of paper goods should not have splatters on them. Your bags should not be greasy. They should not be blowing in the wind and picked up off the ground and used. You should wear gloves. Tongs and deli papers to handle food ungloved are a cheapskate cop out. This shows you put cost savings above cleanliness. I don't care if your state allows it. Set your standards higher or don't bother doing this business.

Your umbrella or tent should be stain and tatter free. Broken handles on utensils should be discarded. Stained cutting boards bleached or resurfaced. Completely set up and then step back and critically look at the overall appearance. Remember you want to move towards the $100,000 profit level and you can't do that with a filthy cart.

QSAC - Atmosphere

Atmosphere for a street vendor is personality based. I am professional, so my atmosphere is just that. If you are comedic than make that your atmosphere. In the early 1980's Mark Caserta joined Rax as a manager and I had the privilege to work with him for a year or so. Mark come to us from Wendy's and really brought a professionalism to Rax I had never experienced. His demeanor commanded respect without intimidation and his results spoke for

Operations

themselves. Mark, at each shift change would make sure the store was in great shape for the coming manager and asked, "Anything I can do for you before I leave?" every single time. Once properly relieved Mark would extend a firm handshake, offer some encouragement for the oncoming manager and crew then take his leave. Mark handled employee and guest alike with optimism, compassion, understanding and consistency.

Mark was promoted and transferred at one point, much to the disappointment of our crew. During the going away party one crew person asked why he had to be transferred and not the store manager (whom everyone felt was a poor manager). Mark was being transferred because the store needed his talents and as a side benefit the new store was significantly closer to his home. Rather than make his answer self-serving or putting down the store manager to bolster his own ego, he told the staff referring to me "you don't take Johnny Bench out from behind the plate." And left it at that. Managers don't win games, it is the players blood, sweat and performance that win. Humble professionalism, calm leadership and hard work was Mark's atmosphere at each store he worked. For me, I'm still working on the humble part.

Having written policies, recipes and procedures will ensure consistency and accountability. For my cart, I have written recipes for every bit of food that I sell. From the Cole slaw and chili recipes to the method of cutting onions, everything has a spec, an expected yield and cost per serve. This is a part of my Operations Manual. This little book sets me apart from nearly all cart vendors and most mom and pop restaurants. Now you may be asking "why waste the time writing something down that probably no one will see?" The act of writing down recipes and food specs helps focus you on delivering quality food while still being profitable. I use this book as part of my presentation when booking a new location, when booking catering and when training my helpers for big events.

Putting the Cart Before the Dog

Professionalism justifies my pricing. It gives my potential clients a sense of security that my food will be delicious, safe and consistent.

Everything you do in business life as well as personal life is being governed by rules. Whether you like the rules or not they exist. Break a rule and you may suffer serious consequences. Cheating on your spouse may only hurt one person but you suffer as well. Your integrity, your honestly and loyalty are now in question. Everything you do in business must be on the up and up. Dishonestly may gain a few dollars but at the cost of your trustworthiness. Live by the personal rule "Everything I do is legally, ethically and morally right." I have always tried to live this rule. If I make an employee a promise I keep it. Even if the business suffers short term from it. Years ago, I had a server that needed to leave the restaurant on a very busy night. I promised if she could just hang in till 7PM I would let her go no matter how busy. She stayed and at 7PM a huge group of people swarmed the restaurant. I kept my promise to her and let her leave. She protested halfheartedly about how busy it would be without her and I just reminded her "I keep my word." She left, and I tried to help the remaining servers as much as possible. From that point forward, she became my best server coming to my rescue many times when other servers called off work. I have dozens of people that will come work for me if I call them. Not because I am an easy manager but because they know they will be treated fairly and honestly.

Disney for all its faults is by far the best company at guest service. Pristine parks, engaged employees and happy guests. They have systems for everything. The operational system governing all aspects of park operations is an easy to remember set of initials: SCSE. Which mean **S**afety, **C**ourtesy, **S**how, **E**fficiency. Every function within a business revolves around those values Same in your food operation.

Operations

Safety for you and the guest (that is why I hate the shin nicking fenders) and of course holding and serving your food in a safe manner.

- I practice safe behaviors in **everything** I do
- I act to always put safety first.
- I speak up to ensure the safety of Others

Courtesy goes beyond an empty smile. It is making a positive connection when your guest asks the same question you have heard a thousand times, rather than rolling your eyes and giving a grumpy ole reply.

- I project a positive image and energy
- I am courteous and respectful to Guests of all ages
- I go above and beyond to exceed Guest expectations

Show is your presentation of food, yourself, your cart. Everything the guest can see, touch or taste.

- I perform my role in high food quality and great service
- I ensure my cart is show-ready at all times

Efficiency is your ability to handle guests in a fast-efficient manner WITHOUT sacrificing the first three.

- I perform my role efficiently so Guests get best food and service possible
- I use my time and resources wisely during slow periods

Check this 2-minute video for a better understanding https://www.douglipp.com/videos/?dzsvg_startitem_vg1=16

Marketing

People are in such a hurry to launch their product or business that they seldom look at marketing from a bird's eye view and they don't create a systematic plan. **Dave Ramsey**

Marketing is something that will make a poor site successful and a great site seem like a cemetery. So how should you market? Social media is a must. Facebook and Twitter at least. Both draw different types of followers. Instagram is another good one if you like taking photos of your food, your set up and your specials.

Use Facebook Business to create ads that are posted on timelines (https://www.facebook.com/business). You pay for only the amount of exposure you can afford. Facebook often set up demo ads with special pricing and limited reach on my page. The ad is usually based on photos, posts and links I've put on my wall. The target reach is 100 to 150 people in your physical area or can be people with similar interests for only $5.00. The ad appears on the targeted persons timeline and hopefully they click to find out about the great food you serve and where you are located. Of course, you

Marketing

can make your own ad and not use the demo at all for the same price.

Cross promote your location especially if you move around from day to day or week to week. Post something like "Today from 11-2 our great dogs are at the corner of 5th and Vine, Saturday we will be at Tom's Hardware on Main." Attach a picture of your set up on 5th or a picture of your best hot dog. Then on Saturday more pictures with that location and the next.

Encourage guests to post photos of themselves enjoying your food. Offer discounts based on the number of "shares", "likes" or "retweets". One promotion I use for new sites is to offer a weekly free hot dog when they share my pre-opening Facebook post, that share gets a certain number of likes AND they purchase a combo meal on opening day they get a card numbered 1 thru 52 with a good till date of one year later. I sign the card to prevent copying. The post looks something like this:

To make this effective and profitable simply post the rules on your Facebook page that include:

- Only 1 Free hot dog redeemed per week
- No other purchase required
- Past missed weeks are lost (no saving up punches)

- Ending date of XX/XX/XXXX (one year from opening)
- Lost cards are not replaced
- Limited to first 30 (or whatever number you feel comfortable) people showing correct "like" count

In practice, this program sees 90% redemption first week dropping to 50 % the third week. By the end of the second month only 15% are being redeemed consistently. By the six-month mark only 1 or 2 a week are redeemed. I see over half order chips and a drink to compliment the free hot dog. The numbers look like this:

If the full 30 guests achieve the like goal and show up on opening day, your business has at MINIMUM 30 different people sharing and from 30 to 870 different people seeing and liking your ad. Only 30 different people "liking" means the same group just circulated ad amongst themselves. 870 means no overlapping of friends at all. In reality, there could be more "likes" simply because some people will fall short of the goal.

30 guests purchasing a $7.00 meal on opening day is worth $210 in gross sales or roughly $116 in profit. In our earlier example, the cost of a chili dog for a vendor is $0.65. Week one cost estimate is $17.55 (27 redemptions). By week 3 it is down to $9.70 (15 redemptions) and by 6 months in it down to $1.30 (2 redemptions). Over the course of the year your food cost for the give-away will run around $200 to $300. Now subtract the original profit of $116 leaves at most $184. If you are a great suggestive sales person, getting 50% to buy something additional like chips, drinks and deserts means the original opening budget for this event is completely paid and likely on the profit side.

If you have a decent following of your own on social media, make sure you promote your business there with links and don't be afraid to ask for your friends and family to do the same. You could even start a YouTube channel with live feeds showing your daily

Marketing

operation, the lines, the food and even your banter with guests. Show a special of the week, in a video, as you demonstrate how you cook and dress the dog on your cart. Offer a discount to someone that shows they subscribed to you. As you are getting ready to open take your phone and shoot a short video showing you in front of your cart saying, "Hey I am open in front of Bob's Hardware on Central Parkway today and I've a chili dog with your name on it!!" Post the video on YouTube and your subscribers get notifications saying you posted a video. That alone is worth it, reminding your guest you exist whether they watch the video or not. Of course, you could even monetize the videos.

Facebook Live videos are given preference in rankings on Facebook. They will show up higher in a person's feed than a picture post or a word only post. Utilize this and post a commercial every day you set up. Again, be funny, witty and charming. Show off your food, location and invite folks down to see you. Maybe even offer a discount for sharing your video.

Instagram is the hot media right now for food vendors. Pictures do the selling for you. You can leverage Instagram and other social media by understanding and then using the "influencers" of your location or city. On Instagram search your city or address if you live in large city. The search will return the 9 most popular posts for that area as well as the most recent posts. Select a mix of recent (because they are active and nearby) and popular posts (they have an audience) and message each one individually. Compliment their profile or pictures and offer them a free signature hot dog (today only) and list your business hours. Set a daily goal of 30 minutes reaching out to influencers. In practice you will see 1 to possibly 7 people out of every ten collect on the free hot dog. Many of those will purchase at least a drink. Dazzle them with your service and make certain the food you serve to them is outstanding in presentation as it will likely be a photograph on their page. In the course of a week you contact 100 people you will get 10 to 30 new guests and of that group at least 1 to 7 will post a photo giving your cart more exposure. Long term you are looking to connect with that significant other of a local celebrity, politician or sports figure that will open many more avenues of revenue for you.

In my cart business, everything is pirate themed. My uniform, for instance, is an emerald green bandana for hair restrain, a baggy renaissance style short sleeve beige shirt and dark brown shorts. I wear black slip resistant shoes. (from Shoes for Crews) I hang a tri-corner hat with a cutlass & scabbard in the back part of my canopy. All for conversation. My food and cart are not easily forgotten. I never sit in a chair waiting for business (it looks bad & guest feel like they are disturbing you). I am up talking to people, offering samples of the **Walkin' d Planks** and generally building relationships for the future. If there is no one around I am near the road waving, pointing to my advertising and just trying to get attention. Ray Kroc, McDonalds founder, is famous for saying "If you got time to lean, you got time to clean!" I have used that a time or two in my restaurant career. As a business owner "If you got time to sit, your business ain't fit!" If you are onsite and sitting down, you are missing opportunities to engage future guests or draw attention to your business. If you are open 3 hours, you should be busy 3 hours. If you need to sit-down all the time, remember, call centers are always hiring!

Use some sort of guest loyalty program. Punch cards where your guests get a free something after purchasing a certain number of the something work quite well. Generally, they are the first thing restaurant managers default to when trying to invigorate sales. Bounce back coupons are useful as well. A bounce back coupon is a coupon you give guests today good for some time in the future. The offers are generally buy one get one (BOGO) or something free with some other full price purchase. Another little promo trick is to place a fish bowl or similar container, seed it with a few other people's business cards and place a sign on the side offering to feed

Marketing

the office (list some limit you are comfortable with) free if their card is drawn. You will gain insight in where your guests are coming from, how to better market to them and their work location.

Printing and passing out flyers is a great way to meet businesses near your location. That is why on the Location Viability sheet you are listing the number of businesses. This makes you take a critical look at your surroundings and maybe notice something you did not know was there. Passing out flyers works and works well if you offer something in return for employees and managers.

- First thing is to design and print flyers.
- Next, list all the businesses and offices you wish to visit. Call each during "slow periods" (I hate when sales people call at lunch) and ask if you may visit bringing treats for employees and flyers for break areas.
- Decide on an offer for the managers and employees that will be on going. Something like "Show your ID badge and get $1.00 off". This could be specific to each business or a blanket offer printed directly on the flyer.
- Purchase the treats. I have used donuts, prepacked cookies or brownies, basically something the employees enjoy and feel like they must give your cart a try. I stay away from hot foods as they cool quickly and then leave negative impressions.

Radio has always been my friend. You can in many markets offer in trade value in exchange for ads or mentions. You can offer to piggy back on live broad casts at car lots, store openings or anywhere your radio station is "on location". I have for has little as 7 combo meals gotten a dozen mentions in a live broadcast. Not only my name but how delicious the food was as the DJ was eating while broadcasting. Drop lunch by the office for the on-air personalities. Talk to a sales rep and be honest with what you want. I tell them straight up, my budget or lack thereof and see what can be worked out. I once fell into a deal where a restaurant pulled out of advertising for a special event that only required a Super Bowl party be carted for free. It had to at least $100.00 retail for the party. My relationship with the radio station led to a month of commercials broadcast10 to 12 times daily whenever the "call-in to win" contest was mentioned. So, my cost was a whopping $35.00 in food cost and two hours of my time for 300 commercials.

On location, you will need at least one sign. It can be as simple as a neatly lettered cardboard sign hanging off your umbrella saying something like "2 hot dogs, chips and a drink only $7.00". This establishes what you sell and how much it costs. A hungry passerby now knows enough to decide to eat with you. Feather signs, lighted arrows, wind socks, yard signs and umbrellas with logos all help define what you are selling and draws attention to you. Set these around as your city allows. Make sure you ask before spending money. Some towns and cities have very strict laws on signage. One town I work will not allow yard signs. The police will pull them up and toss them in the trash. If they remove a second sign you are fined. So, it is better to know the laws ahead of time. Human sign spinners get attention and will drive sales. Anything to draw attention to your location and products. Swooper flags, feather flags, yard signs, Burma-shave style signs all work if positioned correctly and not over done.

Involvement in your community will do amazing things for your sales. My very first event was a "Trash or Treasure" sale held at the National Guard armory. I was a very young manager at Rax and as a part of sales building we were each required to do one community involvement event a quarter. Local businesses got together to raise money for heart disease research. Since Rax already had a reputation for helping fund raise we were approached and I happened to be the manager on duty. They wanted us to sell food and donate proceeds to the event. Easy enough. I talked my boss into us using our name to get donations of food from our

Marketing

suppliers to sell rather than us just use our own inventory. Meaning we could then donate 100% of the sales less employee costs. Rax was out only my time, the booth paid for the 2 employees and suppliers donated all the food, soda and chips. Back then (1981) Coca Cola offered use of a covered food trailer in exchange for the cost of the pre-mix soda. Since times were different and hardly anyone worked on the weekend, Coke dropped off the product and trailer Friday night and would pick it up Monday morning. We held our event Saturday from 10 to 2. Sold only hot dogs with chili, onions, ketchup and mustard, chips and drinks. We gave every guest a coupon book for Rax which saved well more than the cost of the hot dog meal, as well as a free sandwich coupon. Our prices were super cheap $1.00 dogs and fifty cent chips or drink. A whopping $2.00 for a combo. After paying for the 2 helpers and the pre-mix we still donated over $400. (Over $1800 at today's prices) A light bulb went off in my head. Since I worked the closing shift and the trailer wasn't due to be picked up until Monday I could use it on Sunday, make extra money for me and still make my shift by 4pm. I set up at Central Park (because, again, small town with Blue laws in the 80's) by the closed park concession stand. Two hours and $156.00 in profit later my life's course was changed, street vending became my 2nd job.

Be involved in your community. Set up fund raisers. Vend at school functions, PTO meetings, sporting events anything that put your name in front of people. Offer coupons and freebies while raising money for charities. These fund raisers will garner lots of free advertisement and good will, as well as, getting your name and product out in the community. Make sure the group mentions you when talking about their event and includes your name in all print advertising. Find out what is happening in your community and get involved.

Branding is different than marketing. Brand is who you are as a business. Marketing is what you sell. McDonalds has two distinct ad types. One is product related the other is business name related. Remember the ads showing breakfast all day? People sitting around a table at 2 pm enjoying breakfast foods, conversing about how glad they are now that they don't have to miss out on delicious breakfast foods because of a crazy work schedule. This ad markets McDonalds breakfast notifying guests about a change in menu. Branding ads are subtler. Take the ad a few years ago starring a teenager with Downs Syndrome. That ad followed the youngster around preforming his duties and smiling as he passes out a bag of food. No mention of food or specials, just a warm and fuzzy feeling for the viewer associated with the brand McDonalds.

Building a brand is more than a logo and color scheme. It is everything you have read to this point. It is the expectation your returning guest has when purchasing your product. It is the bragging a satisfied guest does when describing your hot dog stand and your service. It is the reputation and character of you and your operation. Wear a uniform, have a clean organized set up, sell delicious food at the best serving temperature. Set up the same way every day, be proud of what you sell. Do not allow mediocre to be your standard. No one brags about average. You set the tone for your business. Smile, be courteous, be fast, sell only hot food hot and cold food cold. **Be *positively* memorable.**

All About You

Be yourself, but always your better self. **Karl G. Maeser**

      Maybe I should have called this READ ME FIRST. Many people read about opportunity and even when presented with a sound plan of action and encouragement they fail to act. Often paralyzed by fear of failure and poor self-esteem they settle for easy and safe. If your current "safe and easy" life means you miss out on seeing your kids play in the big game. Or you run out of money before you run out of month. Or you are just tired of the boss and your job, then give yourself a chance to successful. Start part time. Sell at places where you don't need a fancy cart. Set your life on a path where you are in control not some dude in a suit that only see when something has gone wrong. Unemployed? Read the next chapter and get started today setting your life's course the way you deserve. No internet? Go to the library it is free, research all you want, but at the end of the day ACT. Your family and you deserve it.

      The next couple of pages are self-evaluation questions. Some things to ask yourself before spending a penny on anything.

Putting the Cart Before the Dog

Business ownership is awesome. The freedom with owning a hot dog cart is really beyond description. You want to go fishing, go fishing. You want to see your kid sing at school, guess what you can. Want to make enough money to pay for a trip to Walt Disney World and stay on property. Work a popular festival over a sunny weekend. But and that is a big BUT, it is not for everyone. That does not make you a bad person. It makes you human. You can be successful with hard work and you reap the rewards of your own work. Not a small portion of profits afforded you by your boss. Think about it. The person greeting guests and making the food at McDonalds gets about $10.00 an hour. The CEO that hasn't talked to a guest in years makes millions. Own a cart and you are the cashier and the CEO! You won't make millions, but you will have an amazing life.

As I said before I always thought I was fast when I started working at Rax. The blow to my ego came when on a coupon Friday night during the height of dinner rush, the manager asked me to "sweep the parking lot" and replaced me with a GIRL. Now, don't get me wrong women are absolutely as capable as men, but to an eight-teen year old macho man (give me a break it was the '70's) being replaced by a girl was devastating. I used the embarrassment as motivation to get faster and pushed myself to be the best. I could have run from the embarrassment and never came back from sweeping the lot, but I stayed and pushed myself to be better so never again would anyone replace me on the leading position anywhere.

You need to know your starting point not only as a new vendor but as a new business owner that must deal with the public as a way of earning a living. Once you know where you stand you can then being to improve. Until someone takes you off the prime position because you aren't good enough you will never reach your potential.

All About You

How ready are you to be an entrepreneur?

Personality - Friendly Rank from 1 to 10

        Never met a stranger - 10

        Never met a friend - 1

Optimistic - Your outlook rank 1 to 10

        Glass is half full - 10

        Glass is half empty - 1

Drive to succeed - How motivated are you?

        My Personal bills aren't getting paid - 10

        I am financially set - 1

Flexibility - When a problem arises

        I do whatever it takes - 10

        Now I have an excuse not to do anything - 1

Versatility - Wearing many hats

        If it is to be it is up to me - 10

        I am lazy/do as little as possible - 1

Decisiveness - I make decisions & stick to them

        Decide quickly and correctly - 10

        Procrastination is my name - 1

Working with public - Customer facing job

        Held a job in guest service for years - 10

        Never sold anything to anyone - 1

Putting the Cart Before the Dog

Your score: _____

70 – A perfect score? Not likely! No need to read further you will not succeed, correct self-evaluation is critical to improving yourself and your business. You must be brutally honest.

60-69 – IF you have answered honestly you are right where you need to be to continue and pursue your dream of business ownership. Work on the areas you scored lowest while you start your business.

50-59 – You have some work to do on yourself, but this would not prevent you from being successful. Pick your lowest areas to start improving right away.

40-49 – Depending on the weakness you may want to purse something different. If you scored low on personality and working with the public, I would suggest a business not directly dependent on massive guest interaction or fixing that BEFORE purchasing anything.

39 or less – You should improve your skills in the weakest areas and then seek business ownership. All is not lost, just fix what you need to fix then start your business. Focus on dealing with the public that is critical.

Not matter what you scored you have the ability to improve and adapt your current personality to fit into this industry. IF and that is a big IF you have the proper motivation pushing you. You and do a few small things right now to put yourself on the path to self-improvement. Start learning from professional motivators and speakers that connect with you and your personality. Any of the quotes I have used in this book speak to you? Look up the author and learn from them. Most have book, videos, recording on improving aspects of your life. Simple things like reading in your off time or listening to CD's as you drive to your locations.

All About You

Start with:

See You at The Top – Zig Ziglar https://www.ziglar.com/online-store/books/

How to Stay Motivated – CD series – Zig Ziglar

Zig Ziglar was a well-known motivator, writer and salesperson. His stories are filled with wit and country humor all while making his point. He has written over 30 books and I have been listening and reading since 1979.

At the very least watch this Zig Ziglar video https://www.youtube.com/watch?v=Ae-VJ_lauCw and see his short talk on goals. Your goal of business ownership will thank you!

Disney U – Doug Lipp http://www.douglipp.com/

Disney is well known for guest service. I have stayed at many Disney properties, interacted with dozens of employees in parks, hotels, restaurants and cruise ships. Rarely do they fall short of spectacular guest service. Doug Lipp was a part of the Disney Company and has spent a life time immersed in Disney Guest Service. Learn and apply what he teaches, and you will be successful beyond belief.

Seven Habits of Highly Successful People – Steven Covey

Successful people are always learning, reading and listening. It will make a world of difference in your personal, family and business life!

You can do the same. Where ever you are in life today you can take an action, even a small one and make your life better in the future. And that, my friend, is called hope. Like Zig Ziglar used to say:

IF there is HOPE in the FUTURE, there is power in the PRESENT."

Putting the Cart Before the Dog

Do Whatever It Takes!

Our greatest weakness lies in giving up. The most certain way to succeed is always to try just one more time. **Thomas A. Edison**

Can you handle complaints that are over the top? For example, you accidently put mustard on a "no mustard" request and the person explodes as if you poisoned their dog.

Can you greet strangers as if they are long lost friends? If you treat them right and serve great food, they will be.

Can you be firm but fair during a negotiation? State what you want/need and stick to your cost projections without damaging future business relationships.

Do you see hope in your future? Whatever your situation is today you KNOW it will improve in the future because of things you are actively doing NOW.

Do you handle any setback or problem with confidence knowing you can make it better? There are few perfect days in restaurants and carts are no different.

Can you turn on "hustle" when needed? A line of guests is great but can also be a huge problem if it doesn't move quickly enough.

Are you able to cook, assemble and count money all while "being on stage"? You will wear many hats every day, cook, janitor, accountant, salesman, complaint department, marketing and a ton more.

Are you able to plan and then work that plan? Every projection, every assumption can and likely will be wrong. A good ship's captain makes hundreds of course corrections on the voyage to successfully arrive at the correct port.

Can you handle a baseless complaint? A guest comes to you, shows a 90% consumed dog and tells you "It just doesn't taste right and I want my money back!"

All About You

What would you do if your supplier was out of hot dogs? I have run several different concepts and at one time or another had to tell guests "we are out of XXXX" which, of course, was the main product of the concept.

What would you do if you were busier than expected and ran out of food before you ran out of guests? Projections will be wrong both ways, get used to it. We once had to charter a plane and load it with burger meat from Puerto Rico to St Thomas because we vastly under estimated sales volume for our opening week, using a three-week supply in 5 days.

What would you do if the steam table or grill quit working in the middle of lunch? McDonald's shake machines, Wendy's pressure fryers, Burger King's broilers are all example of equipment that have no back up and can fail. I've ran each concept and have had each fail at lunch.

These are just a few of the questions you need to ask yourself before getting in debt and buying a cart, signing a lease for a location and setting up a commissary. Hot dog carts are fun, hard work and sometimes frustrating, but they are well worth the effort. You put in the effort now and you will reap massive rewards later when you are in operation.

Starting with Nothing

Nothing is more expensive than a missed opportunity. H. Jackson Brown, Jr.

Getting started on any new adventure is scary. Fear of the unknown defeats great dreams and best intentions every day. Excuses are served up faster than a McDonalds cheeseburger on a good day. The biggest excuse is "I have no money" followed closely by "I have no time" and "I don't want to fail". Get over it. You can start with almost nothing in many states. Remember you have to have something to sell. You may actually have enough in your home right now to start this weekend making money.

But, but, but, what? How is it legal? Simple, nearly all states have laws concerning this segment of the food industry and for only $47.00 I'll send you a course to get you started....

Just kidding, I couldn't resist. Some "pros" refer to these laws as loop holes or secrets and dole them out like they are giving you title to a gold mine. The general program you need to search in your state is called "Cottage Foods". These are programs that allow food to be prepared in your home kitchen for sale to the public. The allowed foods are basically shelf stable foods. Meaning they

Starting with Nothing

require no special holding method, they are safe at room temperature. I want to stress each state is vastly different in how to get started, what you can sell and how to label it.

These foods include breads, cakes, cookies, some jams, vinegars, honey, candy and dry goods. In Florida, I can bake a pan of brownies, follow the labeling laws and sell on the side of the road tomorrow after registering to collect sales taxes. No inspections, no health department involvement!

So, taking a Duncan Hines brownie mix like this one https://www.walmart.com/ip/Duncan-Hines-Family-Style-Brownie-Chewy-Fudge-Mix-84-oz/10453172#about-item for $5.83 and then selling the 72-portion yield at a super cheap, impulse buy encouraging $1.00 each is an amazing $66.17 gross profit. Remove the cost of packaging and labels and you just turned $6.00 into $60.00!

Now, with that $60.00 you are going to expand your product line. If you have a bread maker use it to make "artisan" breads, use your oven to bake cookies and brownies while the bread is baking. If your bread maker takes 45 minutes per loaf you still would have 6 to 8 loaves and at $5.00 that $30 to $40 more for the next weekend. Add in the cookie sales and you are off to the cart races as it were.

Find a farmer's market near you and shop there one weekend. See what others are selling, find the cost of a booth and make plans to start selling what your state allows. This way you won't need anything beyond what the market requires.

There are some restrictions, that again vary widely state to state. The total annual GROSS sales are limited, for example. In Florida, $15,000 is the limit. Once you cross that threshold you are considered commercial and need different licenses and permits. Could you live off this? Not really. Could it buy you an amazing cart? Absolutely!

Each state allows different foods to be sold with little to no supervision or government involvement. Funnel cakes, boiled peanuts, pecan logs, water melon, oranges, peaches and popcorn fit into this category in many states. That is why you see them all over as you travel the highways.

Get to know your states laws. They serve to protect the consumer as well as establish guidelines for entrepreneurs.

The following is a checklist to get you started on building your cart fund with cottage foods.

- Use Google and search "cottage foods" and your state. This site is the authority, hands down, on cottage foods. http://forrager.com
- Write down only foods that you can produce in your home. (Meaning you have the ability and the equipment.)
- Find the labeling requirements and make sure you can comply.
- Write down any license or inspections you may need.
- Write down any fees. (Kentucky, for instance, has several fees)
- Find recipes for your products or use your own.
- Find a suitable location, farmers market, side of the road, flea market, etc.
- Spend a day producing your inventory.
- Absolutely plan on running out of inventory before the market closes. Homemade baked good dry out quickly and would not be good enough for sale the next week.
- Ask for estimated attendance. Expect less than 10% to 12% to even stop to see what you are selling. Expect about 10% of that number to buy something. So, on 1000 visitors to the market, only 10 to 12 will buy something from you. However, personality and appealing display will increase your sales dramatically. Samples, don't hurt either!
- Set up on the road side if necessary. Location becomes paramount if you choose this route.

Starting with Nothing

There are other ways to raise money for a cart, marketing and inventory as well. You can use any of the crowd funding sites, like Kick Starter. Just make sure you understand how they pay out the funds, what the fees may be and what is expected of you. If you are allowed to post a video, by all means do it. A video with some humor and planning shows you to be more serious than the others that just write a short "please help me 'cause I need it" story. The more information, pictures and your own personality the better.

Another site is https://www.kiva.org/borrow this is a crowd sourced loan site. It has loaned nearly 1 billion dollars in 83 countries and has an amazing 97% repayment rate! Since this is a loan it is not as easy get yourself posted but is worth the time.

Simply save money yourself. I know, I know, not easy if your already living check to check. Listen to Dave Ramsey on the radio, buy his books or visit his site https://www.daveramsey.com/. He offers plenty of advice on saving, paying yourself first and getting out of debt. His sage advice will also benefit your business finances once you get started.

This site https://www.thepennyhoarder.com/ lists real part time activities and jobs to make extra money, as well as, money saving ideas. I have used the mystery shopper websites a time or two. Easy money!

Of course, there is the standard - bug your family for money. Name a dog after them for incentive!

You could also partner with someone. They could buy the cart and starting inventory as an investment. You could repay the loan with interest each month or offer them a portion of the profits for a length of time. Or you could cart share. Each of you vends certain days or certain events.

Putting the Cart Before the Dog

Find a vendor that operates only a few days a week offer to rent the cart on days they are not already vending. Or offer to vend at off times. For example, if they vend Friday, Saturday and Sunday lunch times you could offer to rent the cart and vend the bar crowds Friday and Saturday night. One kitchen manager I know matches her restaurant job salary working only Friday and Saturday nights in front of dance clubs from 11pm to 2/3am.

On the matter of renting a cart. Some "pros" brag about the money they make just from renting carts. They make money not the renter. Here is the problem they fail to acknowledge. A daily rental fee for the cart is not the only cost. The health department license doesn't cover the renter, unless the renter has training. You are still paying for the food, propane, ice, marketing, paper, cleaning, and site rent. Now consider if you get an inspector from the city or health department. In Florida, the inspector will ask for the last inspection as a second infraction in the same area is double points off. You won't have that inspection and chances are the license history will show **that** as a repeated offense. You could be shut down for something that is not your fault. I doubt you will get a rent refund either!

There is an ad running on Craigslist in South Florida for cart rental at the low, low price of $150 a day with a $2000 damage deposit. You could buy a great used cart for that. Plus, he gives you nothing other than the cart, no site, no food handler licenses or training, nothing. Running the numbers for rental look like this.

Starting with Nothing

Profit and Loss Statement

Income

Gross Sales	$	600.00
Sales Tax	$	33.96
Net sales	$	566.04
Credit Card Sales	$	70.00

Variable Costs

Food and Paper

Open Inv	$	-	
Purchases	$	596.57	
Ending Inv	$	428.57	
Subtotal Food & Paper	$	168.00	29.68%

Operational

Gasoline	$	3.69	0.65%
Propane	$	7.23	1.28%
Cleaning	$	1.48	0.26%
CC Processing fees	$	1.93	0.34%
Marketing	$	1.23	0.22%
Ice	$	2.55	0.45%
			0.00%
			0.00%
			0.00%
			0.00%
Total Variable Costs	$	186.11	32.88%

Fixed Costs

Commissary Fee	$	18.00	3.18%
Telephone	$	3.24	0.57%
Rent	$	18.00	3.18%
Insurance General	$	2.40	0.42%
Licenses/Inspection fees	$	3.58	0.63%
Bank Charges	$	0.72	0.13%
Cart Rental	$	150.00	26.50%
			0.00%
			0.00%
			0.00%
Total Fixed Costs	$	195.94	34.62%
Profit/Loss	$	183.98	32.50%

Breakeven	$	291.93

Putting the Cart Before the Dog

$183.98 in profit may sound like a lot but you will not have that in cash. You have $428.57 in inventory left over for your next day and nothing in positive cash flow. In fact, you still owe yourself $210.62. Getting this cart open for one day cost you a total of $810.92. You will have to loan your business another $89.72 to restock your inventory. Yes, the propane will last well beyond the second day and you may not need more gasoline for the tow vehicle, but do you really want to spend another $150? Realistically you would have to pay the license and insurance for a whole year. So, this is really a very one-sided deal.

If rental is your only way to get your own cart, make sure the rent is under $75 a day **OR** your site will produce over $1000 in sales. Consider rental if the cart owner provides support, training, license coverage, insurance coverage, a location and commissary. At that point, the cart owner is justified in a higher price and likely also invested in your success. A win-win proposal. You will have many of the same costs but the cart owner, by providing a location, needs you to be successful and meeting health standards. Otherwise, he loses a good site and his cart will not retain rental value.

There you have it, a plan to make business ownership a reality and someone to guide you along the way. I will help answer any question, give advice and support on your journey.

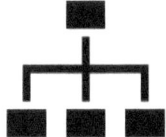

Expansion Time!

Without customers, you don't have a business. You have a hobby.
Don Peppers & Martha Rogers

So true, so true. But what do you do when you are successful enough to live off cart income only? If you can pay for all cart expenses and have enough left over to pay ALL your personal bills, save for the future and play a little, you, my friend, are a business success!

The easiest way to expand is adding hours of operation or expanding your menu. (IF YOUR STATE CODES ALLOW) You could even have a different menu by day part. Breakfast items in the morning and sandwiches and hot dogs for the lunch crowd. Breakfast burritos are super easy to prep and hold. As are biscuit sandwiches. Country ham and sausage are easy and taste great on a grill. Don't have a flat top? No problem Google "boil in bag eggs". This is a product you can cook in your steam table. In minutes, you have 5 pounds of fluffy scrambled eggs. Transfer them to a 1/3 sized pan and hold at 140 degrees. Use an ice cream scooper to portion the eggs, add meat and cheese to your burrito and viola burrito in about 6 seconds serving time. Biscuits are also easy. McDonalds uses a par baked biscuit that takes about 5 minutes to reach temperature in the oven. Brush on butter and it is biscuit time. No oven you say? If your grill is domed rather than a flat lid, guess what you have an oven. It just takes a little experimenting to get the temperature and timing correct. Got left over sausage? Refrigerate and make gravy tomorrow. Breakfast is actually easier for me. Guests are generally on the way to work or school, so they hurry to order, grab condiments and get away. Also, you aren't adding condiments and special requests to everything you sell. This adds an easy $500 additional to your gross sales. Food cost (my target is 23%) tends to run lower for breakfast so more money hits the bottom line.

Expand drink and desert offerings. No, not more variety in sodas and Little Debby cakes. (AGAIN, IF CODES ALLOW) Using the same brownie mix mentioned in "*Starting with Nothing*" increase the serving size to double or triple the recommended size. Using your commissary equipment, bake the brownies and allow to cool. Wrap with food service cling wrap and sell for $4.00 each. A wonderful 6% food cost! Coffees and flavored drinks are all the rage. Take advantage of the fad while it lasts. Iced coffees are super easy and can be flavored adding additional sales and profits. How easy? At BK using the normal coffee, a triple portion is brewed into a single pot. That coffee is cooled and then added to a simple syrup (which you can buy at Restaurant Depot) and water mixture. When ordered fill a cup completely with ice and pour the coffee. Flavor the coffee with chocolate, caramel or other syrups and charge $4.00 or more. Another drink line is flavored citrus drinks. Take a base lemonade, for example, and add raspberry or strawberry syrup or both. Garnish with real lemons or strawberries, charge $3.00 for a 32-oz. cup and have a cool food and paper cost of 17%. There are also vendors that specialize in Lemonades using whole lemons and a

Expansion Time

devise to crush the juice out of the lemon into the serving cup. They add simple syrup, ice and a garnish charging $5.00 per 32-oz. cup.

Don't rest on your laurels now! A single cart allows a certain amount of freedom and financial stability, but the income is capped by your abilities and unfortunately, the weather. How can a vendor hedge against weather, injury or sickness preventing the cart from opening? Increase the number of income streams.

If one cart produces $50,000 after tax income annually, work towards a second cart doing the same sales volume. Then a third cart and so on. I know what you are thinking, how do I staff them? That's why I encouraged you to write procedures and policies in a manual. Now you have the basis for training an employee. I mentioned I am a control freak, so when I hire an employee I have a complete training guide to follow. This ensures the new hire is up to speed and giving the type of quality and service, my guests expect. An employee requires, at minimum food safety training. Check with your health department for your local requirements for food service employees.

Develop some type of bonus or incentive for the employee so that they will be invested in the success of the cart. Structure the bonus program with several different areas to measure performance. I always work my new location and hire someone for my old location. This doesn't task a new employee with trying to build sales all they have to do is maintain what I have developed.

Here is my bonus matrix I use when hire employees. I have used this type of system since 2000. Inspired by Mark Ordway (Burger King Franchisee Vice President of Operations and the most inspiring, principled leader I have ever met or worked with), this matrix system rewards varying levels of desired performance and is not the typical all or nothing bonus system most restaurant companies offer.

Putting the Cart Before the Dog

Bonus Matrix					
% Of net $	3%	1%	0%	-1%	-3%
Sales over LY	5% or more	1% to 4.99%	0 to .99%	-.01% to -4.99%	-5.00% or more
Food cost %	27.99% or less	29.01% to 28%	29% to 30%	30.01% to 31.99%	32% or more
Waste	.4 or less	.41 to .50	.51 to .60	.61 to .69	.70 or more
Attendance	0 trady & 0 absence	1 tardy & 0 absence	2 tardy & 0 absence	3 tardy or 1 absence	2 absence
Mystery Shopper	100	91-99	90	80-89	79<
Last year $	$ 8,548.11	Max Bonus	$ 1,025.77		

Looking at the matrix, you will notice I reward 5 different areas of performance and offer differing levels of rewards. For example, an employee nailed the mystery shop at 100, had no absence or tardy, food cost at 29.5%, waste of .45% but missed sales and was negative 1% would receive a bonus of 6% of net sales or $461 dollars. Add that to the hourly rate I pay of $10.00 and mileage I pay for towing the cart back and forth to the commissary, brings the total pay package to $1436.60. Or a whopping $15.96 an hour! Maxing the bonus on the example sales would yield over $22.00 an hour.

I do all the prep work and clean up for all carts as well as inventory purchasing. My employee meets me at the commissary and gathers up the cart and food to transport to the location. They are on the clock and that is why I offer mileage reimbursement and I can verify tardiness as they must meet me at certain time. The mystery shop could happen at any time and the form I use will fail the visit if the cart isn't open for business on time or is closed early. (The employee must call me to close due to weather) I use friends and regular guests to mystery shop and offer them free food as incentive as well as reimbursing the actual visit cost. Inventory is counted upon return to the commissary and compared to sales reports. Any discrepancy is counted as waste. We then verify sales and reconcile cash to the reports. I use LoyversePOS which provides all the tracking I need as well as security as I can lock employees out of seeing sensitive sales reports. My expectation is the cash matches exactly. If it does not the difference is taken out of the tips jar. We then review sales, food cost and waste. The

Expansion Time

employee knows where he stands bonus wise and what to do to improve. This entire process takes 15 to 20 minutes and the employee is finished for the day. This system has worked well for me. I don't do this all year long as my area is very tourist driven. Spring is college kids and I track what college goes on break when. I know what schools come here and who passes us by. Summer is family time vacation. Once school starts mid-August the prime time is lost, and my additional carts are closed. Fall is slow, and winter is dead between weather and a lack of interest in outdoor activities I may only open 7 to 10 days, if that, each month till March. When I do open it is usually at fairs and flea markets, so I get guaranteed business.

One last item on hiring employees check with the state on rules and regulations pertaining to reporting new hires and your responsibilities with unemployment insurance and workman's comp. Remember to account for those costs.

When you increase your income your state and federal tax brackets will change. Remember to account for the increased tax liability and make those payments on time! As always seek profession advice concerning your taxes.

On the next page is a P&L showing the profit potential of this system. This sample is set up for a one-month sales period. Look at it this way. If you spend 90 minutes a day prepping, inventorying and cleaning your second cart you just paid yourself $115 an hour for just that cart. Amazingly enough, a third cart does not add the full 90 minutes to your day as you will just be prepping in bigger quantities and cleaning only a few more pans. Doubling or tripling carts absolutely does not double or triple prep and clean up time.

Putting the Cart Before the Dog

Profit and Loss Statement

Income

Gross Sales	$	9,061.00
Sales Tax	$	512.89
Net sales	$	8,548.11
Credit Card Sales	$	1,057.00

Variable Costs

Food and Paper

Open Inv	$	-	
Purchases	$	2,664.00	
Ending Inv	$	271.78	
Subtotal Food & Paper	$	2,392.22	27.99%

Operational

Employee Milage $0.35/mile	$	75.60	0.88%
Propane	$	89.28	1.04%
Cleaning	$	18.67	0.22%
CC Processing fees	$	29.08	0.34%
Marketing	$	19.99	0.23%
Ice	$	38.51	0.45%
Employee Labor $10.00/hour	$	900.00	10.53%
FICA	$	68.85	0.81%
Workers Comp	$	23.40	0.00%
Unemployment tax	$	24.30	0.00%
Total Variable Costs	$	3,679.90	43.05%

Fixed Costs

Commissary Fee	$	360.00	4.21%
Telephone	$	45.00	0.53%
Rent	$	250.00	2.92%
Insurance General	$	24.91	0.29%
Licenses/Inspection fees	$	20.67	0.24%
Bank Charges	$	10.00	0.12%
			0.00%
			0.00%
			0.00%
			0.00%
Total Fixed Costs	$	710.58	8.31%
Profit/Loss	$	4,157.63	48.64%

Max Bonus	$	1,025.77
Final Profit after Bonus payout	$	3,131.86

Expansion Time

Cart rental is another income stream method and a way to help a budding vendor get started without the massive upfront expense. Design the contract to be fair to both parties and offer training if the individual requires it. You may need some type of security deposit or require a bond. Don't be like the dude in South Florida that rents for $150 a day plus $2000 security deposit. It does you absolutely no good if the renter stops renting after one day when he figures out he could buy a great cart for $2150 and keep all the profits for himself. Or he realizes that he is not making any money. Remember contracts must be win-win.

Another income stream is to buy and resell used carts. Using the inspection sheet, I gave you negotiate a great deal on the purchase side and you could easily make $500 to $1000 per cart. Simply purchase the cart at a fair, but favorable price. Spend time on cleaning and shining. Repair any issues. Include your recipes, guidance and support as well as any training materials you have. Determine your bottom price for profit and list the cart well above that but lower than a new cart of the same model.

I look for carts that list under $1500. Set an appointment and inspect the cart. If it has small dents and a couple of required repairs, I point them out and offer $750 and go from there. Most likely we settle around $1100 and I take it home. I'll put in the labor to straighten dents and repair whatever needs it. I find the cost of a new one and list mine for 60% of new. So, if new is $3200 I list mine for $2000 knowing my bottom is $1600. Room to allow the purchaser to feel like they got a deal and room for profit. $500 in profit for 3 or 4 hours of inspecting, repair and polishing is a good day in anybody's book. I offer my training material, recipes and ops manual as incentive for a full price offer.

Save money to convert a closed, equipped restaurant into a commissary. Then use the parking lot as rental space for vendors. Bundle the fees into a great deal for you and the vendors. Fees would include commissary usage, space rental and a fee for advertising the lot as a destination for great food from great vendors. Older fast food restaurants have huge land foot prints. Hardee's, for example, big building, big kitchens and huge lots. You could even open the dining room as a common area for seating for the guests of the various vendors. Seattle has what they call food pods for gathering food trucks and vendors in a common area this is a similar idea.

Of course, you could get into cart design and manufacturing. At least three of the major manufacturers in the US have roots as vendors. They tell stories of street vending leading them to help others by manufacturing the best in the industry carts. Well, except they fail to mention the basic cart design is ancient and not work flow efficient. They also seem to "forget" the struggles of starting out by charging crazy high prices for a cart and offering discounts for joining an overpriced "private" training groups. One manufacturer brags about selling his carts to a guy who in turns sells them on ebay. So exactly who is being over-charged? Oh yeah, the end user, the one that needs a deal.

Glossary

8 to 1 – This is an often-used term with many variations. It means 8 of something inside of 1 measurement. For hot dogs, this means exactly 8 hot dogs in one pound. 4 to 1 would be 4 each in one pound. Many foods are "sized" this way. Shrimp, for example, could be sold as 16-20 or 31-35 meaning 16 to 20 per pound, a larger shrimp than the 31 to 35 per pound. In a hamburger restaurant (read McDonalds and BK) the regular cheeseburger is a tiny 10 to 1. Thus, a whopping 1.6 ounces of beef in each patty. :(

Buns – Restaurants often refer to buns as "bread carriers". For us in hot dog vending buns are very important and develop a "signature" for our cart. Side cut is the most common bun used and what most of us associate with a cookout. A 6" long bun cut ¾ of the way through from soft side to soft side. A stale bun will break completely apart and either increase your waste or disappoint the guest if used. A Top cut bun AKA New England Style Roll is the same style bun only cut ¾ way through starting with the crown to the heel. This bun is a little more forgiving when opening as the heel crust helps hold it together. Of course, there are other varieties of buns. Google is your friend.

Catering – This is an opportunity to make additional money beyond daily sales. For example, a company wants to hold its picnic at a state park and wants the food end of the picnic handled by someone other than employees. They rent your cart and employ you for the food service. Since this is a private event you can now prepare foods you don't normally sell. They are paying you for a set amount for time and for food. All the left-overs (if any) belong to the company. For 3 hours of work you can gross $2000 or more! This could be your only work day every month if you wanted that.

Cold Holding - An area on your cart that holds back up meat and condiments at a temperature of less than 41 degrees. This is obtained usually with ice and monitored with a thermometer.

Commissary - may provide anything from a source for obtaining potable water and disposing of wastewater; storage for food and supplies; provide area for cleaning of pots, pans and utensils; or cooking facilities to prepare the food for sale and consumption.

DBPR - Department of Professional and Business Regulation. One of two agencies that monitor, inspect and approve street food vendors. The other is the Department of Agriculture. They each inspect different business types. In Florida, your commissary must match the license type you have. Other areas of the country call this the Health Department or similar name.

EIN - An Employer Identification Number (EIN) is also known as a Federal Tax Identification Number, and is used to identify a business entity. Generally, businesses need an EIN. You may apply for an EIN in various ways, and now you may apply online.

Fictitious Name - Law vary from state to state. In the case of a corporation, a fictitious business name is any name other than the corporate name stated in its articles of incorporation. If you're starting a sole proprietorship or a partnership, you have the option of choosing a business name or dba (doing business as) for your businesses.

FIFO - Restaurant jargon pronounced fi - foe or First In First Out - meaning First product in must be first product used. This insure fresh product and reduces waste or spoilage.

Fixed Cost - Total of all costs that do not change regardless of business volume. For example, license fees, rent, basic phone service, insurance, monthly bank fees. These all must be paid whether you are open for business or not.

Glossary

Food safety classes - These are classes your local Health Department will require you to take. You will learn the basics of food safety, proper storage, proper hot holding/cooling as well as bacteria associated with different foods. Often you are given a grace period after opening to get your certification. If you have never worked in food service do this before opening so you don't develop poor habits and standards before you know better.

Guest - Restaurants refer to their customers as guests. Your advertising 'invites' them into your business. When you are inviting people to your home for a cookout or party, you as a good host makes sure everything is clean, ready and perfect for your guests. The bar is lower for 'customers' because that is a faceless entity that seems easy to replace with another faceless entity. Salesmen tend to think of customers as a $ sign. Salesmen say anything to close the sale, brag on non-existent quality, promise delivery dates that don't materialize, offer useless add-ons to increase commissions. Restaurant owners depend on guests they will see often and if you are good very often!

Hand Washing- From the CDC:

- **Wet** your hands with clean, running water (warm or cold), turn off the tap, and apply soap.
- **Lather** your hands by rubbing them together with the soap. Be sure to lather the backs of your hands, between your fingers, and under your nails.
- **Scrub** your hands for at least 20 seconds. Need a timer? Hum the "Happy Birthday" song from beginning to end twice.
- **Rinse** your hands well under clean, running water.
- **Dry** your hands using a clean towel or air dry them.

Think about this on your next doctor or dentist visit!

Putting the Cart Before the Dog

Hot Dog Vendor – A street vendor that is only allowed to sell precooked frankfurters. Often states also prohibit cooking of any type on these carts. For example, heating chili or cooking onions are not allowed. No cooking of any raw foods.

MFDV – Mobile Food Dispensing Vehicle which can sell more than just hot dogs. A MFDV can be a cart or a food truck.

P&L – Short for Profit and Loss statement. This is the accounting term for a report that reflects all financial data relating to the business. Listing all income and removing all expenses leaving either a profit or a loss on the bottom line.

QSAC – Short for Quality, Service, Atmosphere and Cleanliness.

Servicing Area – The FDA name for "commissary". A food establishment that a mobile unit uses to store food, clean equipment and possibly store their unit.

SOS – Short for Speed of Service. Most restaurants set standard for SOS and measure it with radar, timers, computers or stop watches and observation. For example, McDonalds uses timers built into the cash register and order monitors thru out the kitchen and order assembly areas.

Steam Table – This is a pan or piece of equipment that holds water that is heated to create steam. Inside of this pan are smaller pans containing the food needing to be kept hot. The smaller pans are named after the fraction of the whole pan. Thus a "full size" pan is the whole while a "third size" is 1/3 of the "full size". The bottom number of the fraction explains how many of these pans fit in the steam table. Common sizes are full, ½, 1/3, ¼, 1/6 and 1/9. To further complicate things each pan as varying depths such as 2 ½, 4, 6 and 8 inches. Steam tables also require spacer bars. These bars are often mistakenly described as only needed to support the smaller pans. They actually are needed to contain the steam inside

Glossary

the full-size pan rather than venting the steam away from the hot food and allowing the pan to boil dry. Steam tables are **not safe** to reheat leftover foods as the reheat cycle takes far too long. In order for the food being held to remain hot and the water not boil away the food pan must sit down 2 inches inside the water. Water transfers heat more efficiently than steam. For more information https://www.katom.com/cat/hotel-pans-food-pans/guide-steam-table-pan-sizes.html

Variable Cost – Listed as a percentage. These costs increase in dollars as sales increase, but the percentage is consistent. For example, food cost of 30% will be 30% at $100 or $1000. The dollars spent, of course, are $30/$100 or $300/$1000.

Vendor Program – Food manufacturers often have programs designed to assist resellers with marketing their products. Sometimes deeply discounted or even free, you can get food, banners, signs, t-shirts, hats basically anything with a logo to advertise the brand.

Excuses, excuses

Ninety-nine percent of the failures come from people who have the habit of making excuses. **George Washington Carver**

Thank you for reading this far! I am impressed! 57% of all books purchased are never finished and a scary 42% of college graduates will never read a book after they graduate. The fact you are almost done is amazing. The next item on your agenda is to put your reading to work and act to achieve your food dream.

Now to make this a complete circle let's talk about quitting, giving up and being a loser. Everyone that starts something new like weight loss or exercise will start out like a house on fire and eventually hit a wall and progress slows or stops. Then depending on the person, either digs deeper to succeed or gives up using some form of loser's limp. We all know the loser's limp, the guy chasing the leader pulls up, limping, allowing the score or someone else to win the race. Don't be that person. But if you must, I prepared a list of excuses to save you time 'cause I like helping people. (I also include my rebuttal)

Excuse, excuses

I have no money. **Did you even read the *Starting with Nothing* chapter?**

Manager says "corporate" says NO. **Did you talk to corporate yourself?**

I talked to corporate and they say no. **Is that the only business in town? Ask again!**

I can't get into any local fairs they have cut off all food vendors. **Apply for next year's fairs today!**

I can't find a commissary. **Really? There are no restaurants, bars, stores or churches in your town? See what it takes to start your own.**

I can't find a business that wants a food vendor? **Did you try all the public venues like government offices, court houses, state and city parks?**

My health, my back, my legs, my blah, blah, blah is not good enough to do this business. **You have a choice to make... live or die. I've been there, and I refuse to give in to pain.**

My wife, husband, mom, dad, bf, gf says I can't succeed at this. **Are they experts in the food industry? Have they run a cart?**

I can't find a cart to vend from. **Cottage foods my friend. Cottage foods.**

I am shy. **Me too. I just like eating and a roof over my head more than the fear of people.**

My first day I made nothing. **Better site, Better advertising, Better food, Better service. It is all in your control.**

My first month and I am still struggling. **Email me pictures, video and your city and location so I can look it up on Google Street View. I will help you.**

Putting the Cart Before the Dog

Did you notice each excuse is linked by one common trait? Do you know what every successful person in history in some way, shape, form or quote insists that you need to become successful yourself? **Perseverance.** The ability and personal drive to not give up when things get tough. Imagine if your parents stopped encouraging you to walk after that first tumble or if they stopped repeating words over and over and over to get you to say "mama" or "dada". If you care about yourself, your own security and your success, the way a parent cares about their child's development and future, then keep asking the questions until you get the answer you need to succeed. You deserve it.

Once some people get open they congratulate themselves for getting that far and then stop improving, researching and analyzing. These folks think that the hard work is over, that just by showing up and being open droves of hungry people will be lined around the cart. I talk to people that are selling carts all the time. They got approvals, opened for business and are now selling the only business asset they own, the cart. During the conversation, I ask them "why are you selling?" No matter what they respond, I eventually ask, "why do you think other hot dog carts are going out of business?" This phrasing of the question relieves the selling cart owner of trying to convince me that business is great, running a cart is easy and I should buy their cart. Now rather than focusing on selling, they focus on giving advice to be successful or what to avoid. Likely also telling me how **they** failed under the guise of "the other guys did this, but not me." Excepting for the health related and retirement, I grouped these together by common theme. Several will overlap, and a few were offered by several different people and listed in different categories. As you read these excuses think of ways to prevent the same thing happening to you.

Excuse, excuses

Lack of Knowledge

- "They don't understand the food service industry."
- "…lack of knowledge of the restaurant business, health codes, and city permit laws"
- "…lacked a plan."
- "…very cheap to get started and was not prepared for small business ownership."
- "…no background in the restaurant industry"
- "Lack of planning"
- "Mismanagement of finances & taxes"
- "Realization of exactly how difficult this business is…"
- "lack of understanding of food cost management and time and labor management"
- "The lack of a well thought out business plan"
- "critical business planning, setting real expectations"
- "saturated market"

Marketing

- "I think people are under the impression that if you set up anywhere, people will just show up."
- "You have to be where they work, shop or play"
- "…not using Social media, no Website and not enough new business contacts"
- "lack of promotion"
- "Marketing and promoting is essential"
- "…they do not promote themselves enough"
- "consistently building a customer base"
- "Not understanding how seasons affect business"
- "successful carts are the ones whose customers know exactly where they will be at all times"
- "lack of Location Updating on Twitter and Facebook"
- "boring or uninspired theme or marketing"

- Workload Vs Income
- "...people underestimate the amount of work involved"
- "costs are underestimated"
- "expenses outweigh sales"
- "Low average ticket resulting in low profits.
- "They are not prepared to work so hard for so little and throwing in the towel"
- "over saturation in the market"
- "costs are underestimated."

Menu

- "...fail because they spread themselves too thin".
- "know your competition"
- "takes too long to prepare and is too expensive" "Prices are too high for the amount of food/quality of food"
- "quality of your food slip or the portions shrink"
- "they serve too many options"
- "their menu may be too high priced"
- "...inconsistency"

Service

- "that food has to be served in a timely manner"
- "cannot handle volume"
- "employees are rude to customers"
- "too long to deliver food to customers"
- "bad customer experiences."
- "trying to handle too large of event"
- "not bringing enough food"
- "having too much food causing expensive losses"
- "quick transaction times."

Excuse, excuses

If you notice each excuse should have been addressed in real time. Had these folks just written a well-researched business plan they would have not been talking to me about selling.

Re-read the excuses and think about how you can avoid these mistakes when you write your business plan. Mistakes will be made, and everything is fixable. Had the owners simply been analyzing their own performance each day they would have never been talking to me. You must ask yourself everyday how can I get better and make my business more profitable, grow sales, provide better SOS and satisfy my guests. Make a list and set goals to fix every problem when you encounter it. Wishing away a problem will not work and ignoring a problem is as good as putting a "FOR SALE" sign on your cart.

Thirty something years ago, the list, for me, was usually way too long to even admit. Still today issues arise, service doesn't go smoothly as it should, and I actually know what I am doing. In each and every case had I done more research, paid more attention to the warning signs or just preformed at my best things would have been better.

When you admit and accept responsibility for your mistakes, then begin working on improving <u>and</u> correcting those mistakes, you will, one day soon, be able to celebrate the success of your labors!
Bill Moore

Thank you for reading please email if you have any questions. I'll help you get going and be successful. No group to join, no super-secret outlaw group to hide behind, no buy now button, no 7-day free trial. The most successful restaurants are always training employees and management. Amazingly, not a one of them charges the staff or management to be trained. You should not be charged or basically robbed of your hard-earned money to get "insider pro tips". People selling admission to such groups have no value, no tips and nothing but promises of over hyped information. They even hint at business "secrets" they don't want the masses to know. There aren't any. The super-secret marketing plans or secret family recipes to make your tongue beat your lips for a taste don't exist either. Any decent chef with a good palate can tell you is in a product and how to reproduce it. Besides tastes are regionally defined and a national group offering a recipe can only speak to its reception within their own area.

I won't link you to an article that only links you to another article that only links to a video that links to another article that is really an ad to sell you a course that doesn't tell you anything that I already have for free. If you don run across something that I have not addressed here call me I give you the information without hype and without cost.

My email is **Bill_Moore@live.com** and my direct phone line is **(850) 888-3121** call me any time from 11AM CST to 9PM CST. I will answer questions, offer advice, alter the sheets to fit your needs or anything cart business related you need. The final page has all the links I have mentioned throughout the book.

Resources

Links

FDA:
https://www.fda.gov/Food/GuidanceRegulation/RetailFoodProtection/FoodCode/ucm122814.htm
https://www.fda.gov/downloads/Food/GuidanceRegulation/RetailFoodProtection/FoodCode/UCM577858.pdf

Facebook Business:
https://www.facebook.com/business

YouTube
https://www.youtube.com/channel/UCjQJV8DITRWvAJMngnfTZ9w
Site Checklist https://youtu.be/i87OORfYaOo
Expense Tracking https://youtu.be/gPUzZ8BbT1s

Street Eats Limited:
http://www.bestvendors.com/wp-content/uploads/2017/02/street-eats-application.pdf
http://www.bestvendors.com

Blog and spreadsheet downloads:
https://moorebetterperformance.weebly.com/downloads.html
https://moorebetterperformance.weebly.com/performance-blog/do-i-need-a-sole-proprietorship-or-llc-for-my-food-vending-business

Information on pans sizes:
https://www.katom.com/cat/hotel-pans-food-pans/guide-steam-table-pan-sizes.html

Extra Income:
https://www.thepennyhoarder.com

Self-Improvement:
https://www.daveramsey.com
http://www.douglipp.com
https://www.douglipp.com/videos/?dzsvg_startitem_vg1=16
https://www.ziglar.com
https://www.youtube.com/watch?v=Ae-VJ_lauCw
https://www.stephencovey.com/

Cottage Foods:
http://forrager.com

Point of Sale (POS)
https://loyverse.com
https://squareup.com

Insurance:
https://www.fliprogram.com/
http://insuremyfood.com/food-cart-insurance
https://www.foodsafetymagazine.com/magazine-archive1/aprilmay-2013/maximizing-insurance-coverage-for-food-contamination-claims

Food Safety/Allergen
http://www.mass.gov/eohhs/docs/dph/environmental/foodsafety/allergen-awareness-vendors.pdf
http://allertrain.com/
https://www.servsafe.com

Equipment Auctions
https://www.pciauctions.com

Events
https://festivalnet.com/index.html
https://www.fairsandfestivals.net/

Resources

Florida specific (your state may have one too)
http://www.floridafairs.org/p/6

Commissary
http://www.culinaryincubator.com
https://www.yourprokitchen.com
http://www.icyprofits.com/commissaries.htm
http://www.cookithere.com/

Distributors
http://www.sysco.com/
http://www.cheneybrothers.com/
http://www.fsafood.com/
http://rfsdelivers.com/
www.usfoods.com
https://www.gfs.com
https://totalfood.com/food-distributors/

Whopper Challenge
http://www.mywnynews.com/arcade_warsaw/people/spotlight_on/article_cf4dcf18-2c5d-11e3-a512-001a4bcf887a.html

Speed of Service
http://www.nrn.com/technology/mcdonald-s-focus-speed

www.ingramcontent.com/pod-product-compliance
Lightning Source LLC
Chambersburg PA
CBHW030942180526
45163CB00002B/673